making your family work

making your family work

mary g. durkin

Thomas More Press
Chicago, Illinois

Cloth ISBN 0-88347-224-4
Paper ISBN 0-88347-225-2

Contents

Introduction   1

Part One: Dos and Don'ts For Family Ties

1   Family Ties Skills Test   9
2   Try To Understand   20
3   Be A Good Talker   23
4   Be An Active Listener   26
5   Be Positive   29
6   Give Respect   32
7   Be A Creative Fighter   35
8   Be A TLCer   38
9   Celebration Time   41
10   Apologize, Forgive & Forget   44
11   Give And Receive   47
12   Self-love And Family Pride   50
13   Learn To Laugh   53
14   Don't Triangle   56

15	Don't Blame	59
16	Don't Manipulate	62
17	Seek Help	65
18	A Family Ties Skills Review	68

Part Two: Stresses, Strains, And Supports

19	Till Death Do Us Part	73
20	The Big One?	78
21	Severing The Bond	83
22	What About The Children?	88
23	Separated Parenting	93
24	Stepping	98
25	A Woman's Work Is Never Done	103
26	A Man's Place Is In The Home?	108
27	What About The Children? Part II	113
28	We No Longer Need Your Services	118
29	Grandparents To Love	123
30	Planning For The Golden Years	128
31	Passing On The Dream	133
32	Mother, Make Him Stop	138
33	The Aftermath Of A Revolution	143
34	A Rebel In The House	148
35	New Adults In The Family	153
36	Telling The Family Secret	158

| **A Not So Final Word** | 163 |

In Memory of My Parents
Grace and Andrew Greeley
Who worked at making their family work.

Introduction

The family is a school for relationships. Along with providing food, shelter, and clothing, the family teaches its members how to get along with each other. Just as importantly, the family teaches you how to get along with people outside the family circle. Growing up in a family, the most important lesson you learn is how to build ties with other people.

If you look at the American family in the 1980's as a school for relationships, then two facts are obvious: Some families work; other families don't work. Here, work means something akin to what psychologists call healthy functioning. A family *works* when its members know how to relate to each other in positive, healthy ways. A family doesn't work when its members can't get along or have difficulty dealing with others outside the family.

1

Consider four television families of the 80's. The difference between the Huxtables and the Ewings is much more than the dissimilarity between a relatively young, black family of a Philadelphia doctor and lawyer and an older, rich, white Texas oil family. So, too, the difference between the Keatons and the Carringtons is more than the contrast between a family of teenagers and an adult family. The real difference is that, as a school for relationships, the Huxtable and Keaton families work and the Ewing and Carrington families don't work. The Huxtables and the Keatons are able to deal with difficulties in the family and with problems outside the family. The Carringtons and the Ewings lack this ability.

Your family doesn't have to be a perfect family to be a family that works. The story of one self-proclaimed perfect family proves there is no such thing as a perfect family. While other families struggled with the inevitable problems of family life, this family claimed it didn't have any troubles. Everything the parents did—from parenting to jobs to vacations to leisure activities—was the *only* way to do things.

According to the parents, their children were the brightest, the best looking, the best dressed, the best behaved, the most cooperative, and the most popular. The parents bragged about how well their children got along with each other and with everyone else. For their part, the children lorded their family's superiority over their playmates. Needless to say, outsiders did not share this family's upstanding view of itself.

The family wouldn't leave room for imperfection in any of its members. Eventually, it became a power keg of denied problems, just waiting to explode. A series of minor explosions, rather than one major one, finally forced the family members to acknowledge their family's shortcomings.

Unfortunately, they lacked the skills for dealing with this blow to their image. Because they had denied the existence of problems, they hadn't seen the need to work on their relationships. Today, the family still doesn't function well because its members still don't work at getting along with one another. As a result, they aren't able to face problems in other relationships.

The Huxtables and the Keatons are not perfect by any means. Their stories are about families trying to work out their differences and—at the same time—be useful members of society. Their secret to success is that they work at making family work.

Making Your Family Work is a book for people who want to make their families work and who are willing to work to achieve that goal. If you are like most people, there are days when you want to throw in the towel and run away from the difficulties of trying to live with your family. At other times, you probably wonder how you and your family can cope with all the outside pressures. Then, there are the times when everything goes right. When that happens, you want to shout for joy about the wonders of a family that works.

To make your family work in the 1980's, you must build

family ties that capitalize on the good possibilities of family life and ease the inevitable conflicts. Working on healthy relationships is an ongoing, crucial task for creating good family ties. These ties will then support members when they deal with the stresses and strains of our modern society.

Making Your Family Work is a guidebook for use in the family school. Part One considers the principles for building and maintaining good relationships in a family. These are the family ties skills—the dos and don'ts parents must follow with each other and with their children.

The family school for relationships operates on the following basis: Parents are models for their children, showing them how to behave towards others. Children learn more from what their parents do than from what they say. As children grow older, they relate to other people according to the principles they've learned by observing their parents. Teens and young adults work at new relationships based on the lessons they've learned in the family school.

Even if your family acts as a good school for relationships, it still can be torn apart by outside social pressures. According to the media, the family of the 80's is in big trouble. You probably know many families with problems unrelated to how the family members get along. You might wonder what difference it would make to your children if you taught them about relationships. After all, won't they have to face all the harmful pressures of the modern world? You might even feel that all your work on family ties could prove useless against these influences.

Part Two of *Making Your Family Work* looks at the effects on the family of some of the stresses, strains, and strengths of the contemporary world. You will see how people cope with today's world based on how their family works at relationships. You will find suggestions about how to overcome some present-day obstacles to good relationships. And finally, you will learn that the modern world has some strengths that can help build good family ties.

Making your family work will take work on your part. When you consider what happens when a family doesn't work, the effort seems well worth it. You might not want to be like any of the four television families. If you had to choose, however, wouldn't you rather be part of a family that works?

Part One:
<u>Do</u>s and <u>Don</u>'ts

The Family Ties Skills Test

Making your family work takes work. If you want to be successful, you need basic relationship skills. Before examining the principles for building good family ties, you should examine your present level of skill. The family ties skills test helps you see how well you're doing at this time. It also gives you an opportunity to think about the skills covered under the Dos and Don'ts.

Read each of the following statements and check the answer that best describes how you might react in these situations or how you have reacted in similar instances in the past.

1. *When someone in my family comes to me with a problem, I:*
   (a) always take time to learn all the details about

the problem and try to find out how the person feels because of it.

(b) am sympathetic but don't usually ask for many details.

(c) want to help but am so busy I can't afford to spend much time worrying about someone else's problem.

(d) usually figure the person is making too much of whatever happened.

(e) avoid getting involved because I don't like to deal with other people's problems.

2. *When I need to discuss an important matter with someone in my family, I:*
(a) examine my feelings on the subject and try to express what I think and feel as honestly as I can.
(b) usually blurt out my ideas and feelings in a disorganized way.
(c) find it difficult to be at ease because I am afraid to let my true feelings show.
(d) don't think it's necessary to let the other person know how I feel about what we're discussing.
(e) prefer to write a note or letter, outlining the problem.

3. *Your fifteen-year-old daughter brings up the subject of her curfew. Which of the following best describes how you would react?*
(a) I'd give her an opportunity to explain how she

feels about her present curfew and why it should change. I'd try to understand what was behind her request and, even if I didn't agree, try to make her know I appreciate how she feels.

(b) I'd listen to what she has to say but would probably not understand why she feels as she does.

(c) I'd agree to the discussion but would be sure my decision was right so I would pay little attention to her views.

(d) I'd know this was just another one of her attempts to cause trouble and would give her a lecture on the burdens of parental responsibility.

(e) I'd be angry that she was questioning my decision and would tell her there was no point discussing the idea since I'd already made up my mind about what was best for her.

4. *Whenever I get a bad report on my child's behavior I:*

(a) always consider how this fits my child's usual behavior before deciding what to say; begin discussing the problem with some favorable comments about my child's usual behavior; and listen to my child's side of the story.

(b) immediately demand an explanation from my child but, because of my frustration, find it difficult to listen to his or her side of the story.

(c) lecture my child on how this fits a pattern of misbehavior.

(d) get upset because I can't think of any redeeming qualities about my child.

(e) figure it is just one more sign of how bad things are in the family.

5. *Your son, a high school senior, decides to join the army after graduation. You wanted him to go to college and become a professional. Which best describes how you would react?*

(a) I'd listen to the reasons for his decision; ask him to give serious thought to my reasons for disagreeing; and then realize the final decision—and its consequences—are up to him.

(b) I'd accept that he wasn't a good student but would tell him there was no future for someone who didn't go to college.

(c) I'd tell him that I knew what was best for him and that he didn't have the sense to make a decision about his future.

(d) I'd become upset and continually remind him what a disappointment he was to me.

(e) I'd threaten to disown him if he didn't follow my advice.

6. *Your husband calls from the airport in another city, saying he missed his flight. He'd been trying to change the customer's mind on a big contract. Unfortunately, he was unsuccessful and lost the big commission he was expecting. His disappointment*

is obvious. He'll be home for dinner, but not until after nine o'clock. When he arrives home, which of the following might you do?

(a) I'd fix his favorite foods, serve a candlelight dinner and let him talk about his disappointment.

(b) I'd give him a warmed up meal, ask a few questions about the contract, and then move on to a discussion of other family matters.

(c) I'd tell him I was sorry and then begin talking about all the back-to-school bills that need paying.

(d) I'd complain because his late arrival made me miss my bridge game.

(e) I'd berate him for not working hard enough to get the contract.

7. *For your wife's fortieth birthday what would you do?*

(a) I'd get our children to help me plan a surprise party and invite all her friends and relatives.

(b) I'd take her out to dinner like I do every year on her birthday.

(c) I'd buy her a present and card.

(d) I'd forget it was her birthday until someone reminded me.

(e) I'd do nothing special because I don't like celebrations and making a big fuss.

8. *You had a hard day at the office, stopped after work for a drink with a co-worker, forgot you had prom-*

ised to go to your son's soccer game, and then came home and were short with your husband and children because they asked where you were. Which best describes what happens next?

(a) You realize how wrong your behavior was. You then call the whole family together and you tell them you are sorry without making any excuses for your behavior. You promise to try never to repeat your actions. At the end of the discussion, you make a batch of fudge for everyone.

(b) Your family remains angry with you, so you begrudgingly apologize. But you don't promise not to do the same thing again.

(c) You apologize only after your husband tells you your behavior was improper.

(d) You act offended because they don't appreciate how tired you are at the end of a busy day.

(e) You sulk because the others are mad at you, but you don't think you should have to apologize to your family.

9. *You are the husband in the above story. Your wife apologizes and promises not to act this way again. How would you respond?*

(a) You accept her apology and never again even think about the hurt she inflicted on you and the family.

(b) You accept the apology but can't help thinking about how thoughtless she was.

(c) You accept her apology; but you add this offense to your private scorecard of her shortcomings and refer to it in later disagreements.

(d) You give only halfhearted acceptance to her apology and continue to show her you are still angry.

(e) You refuse to accept her apology, telling her that her behavior is just one more sign of her irresponsibility.

10. *If you find that you are always the one to do all the family chores, how would you deal with the situation?*

(a) I'd call a family conference to discuss how people might share family responsibilities on a more equal basis. I wouldn't make everyone unhappy by complaining about all the work I do for them.

(b) I'd assign chores to people but not tell them why I'm doing it.

(c) I'd suggest that it might be nice if people helped me once in a while.

(d) I'd complain about how unfair it is that I have to do everything.

(e) I'd consider it my duty to do all the chores and would expect them to be grateful for what I did.

11. *Which of the following best describes how you feel about your role in building family relationships?*

(a) The survival of the family does not depend on

me alone. I must allow others to make a contribution to the family and to give me love and support.
(b) I try to think of the needs of others; but sometimes it is difficult.
(c) I just don't have much time to worry about my spouse and children.
(d) I expect my spouse and children to put my needs before theirs without complaining.
(e) I am the most important person in the family. My spouse and children owe me more attention than they give now.

12. *How do you feel about your family?*
(a) I have a good family. We have our ups and downs, and no one is perfect. Still, the good times outweigh the bad, and I'm happy with my family.
(b) My family is pretty good. There is lots of room for improvement; but I'm not sure any changes will ever happen.
(c) My family is O.K., but it can't compare to most other families.
(d) My family would be O.K if a few people would behave better.
(e) I'm ashamed of my family.

13. *When my spouse and I are having problems in our marriage, I usually:*
(a) try to work out the problem with my spouse.

Not wanting my children to take sides, I avoid telling them the details of the disagreement.

(b) let the children know I'm feeling hurt but don't expect them to rally to support me.

(c) hint to the children that I treat them better than my spouse does in the hope they will support me and make me feel better.

(d) make sure all the children know that my spouse is unfair to me and to them.

(e) tell my side of the story to my favorite child, knowing he or she will support me.

14. *The problems in my family are:*
    (a) sometimes my fault; sometimes someone else's fault.
    (b) sometimes my fault.
    (c) usually my fault.
    (d) usually someone else's fault.
    (e) always someone else's fault.

15. *You and your husband have just had a big fight. He settles behind the newspaper and is reading the comics when he finds a cartoon making fun of the same problem that led to your fight. If he were to show you the comic strip, how would you react?*
    (a) I'd join in his laughter over the comic and admit to him how ridiculous our fight was.
    (b) I'd laugh at the comic, and I'd feel less certain

that our fight was worth the energy I'd put into it.
(c) I'd laugh at the comic but wouldn't change how I felt about our fight.
(d) I'd get even madder because he was seeing some humor in our fight.
(e) I wouldn't even look at it. I don't read the comics.

16. **When your spouse and children don't let you have your way, how do you react?**
(a) I try to understand why they find my demands unreasonable and negotiate changes with them.
(b) I think they are being unfair but know I can't change them.
(c) I sulk for a while but realize I can't win against all of them.
(d) I try to figure out a different way of getting what I want from them.
(e) I refuse to love them until they see things my way.

17. **If you knew that you or someone in your family had serious problems that were destroying the family, what would you do?**
(a) I'd check out alternative professional and self-help groups to help me deal with the problem. If another person had a problem, I'd encourage him or her to seek help, too.

(b) I'd read some self-help books.
(c) I'd talk it over with a friend or neighbor.
(d) I might consider getting outside help, but wouldn't follow through and get it.
(e) I wouldn't even consider counselling.

Scoring
Give yourself: 4 points for every (a) answer checked. 3 points for every (b) answer checked. 2 points for every (c) answer checked. 1 point for every (d) answer checked. 0 points for every (e) answer checked.

Your Family Ties Skills Rating
52-68 — You're a family ties expert! Do you know why? Read on! 35-51 — Welcome to the crowd! You're good at family ties; but there's room for improvement. 18-34 — You need help to become more sensitive to building family ties. 0-17 — You need basic training in building family ties!

Read on to discover sixteen family ties skills. These Dos and Don'ts suggest rules to keep in mind as you work at making your family work. Remember these rules and your school for relationships will be a success.

2

Try to Understand

Good communication is the key to good family relationships. To be successful in building family ties you must try to understand family members' real needs, even if they don't talk about them.

At some time in your life, you were probably a character in a dialogue that went like this:

Child: Mom (or Dad), can I go to the rock concert this weekend with my friends? Parent: No, you're too young to go to one of those big concerts. Child: *But everyone else's parents have said it's O.K. Parent: I'm not responsible for everyone else, only for you. Child: Even Mrs. Jones is letting Bill go and you know how strict she is. Parent: If Mrs. Jones says it's all right for Billy to eat rat poison, would you want me to let you eat it? Child: But why can't I go? Parent: Because I said so. Child: You never let me have any fun.*

This short parent-child dialogue demonstrates how lack of understanding leads to problems in family communication. Though the parent and child are talking to each other, neither one understands what the other *really* means. As a result, if you are the child, you feel your parent doesn't want you to enjoy yourself.

More than likely you will sulk the entire time your friends are at the concert. If you're the parent, you're probably angry, too. You wonder why your child can't understand that "everybody's doing it" doesn't eliminate your parental responsibility. Yet perhaps your child doesn't understand because you rely too heavily on parental authority to explain your decisions.

Remember being the child in this conversation? You knew you were really trying to say how important it was for you to be part of the crowd, to feel accepted by others. Your parent's refusal left you open to criticism from your friends. You were convinced your parent didn't understand you. At some level, though, you also knew you were trying to manipulate your parent to let you do something objectionable.

The lack of understanding in this parent-child dialogue is present just as often in husband-wife, parent-child, or sister-brother communication. Unless you try to understand not only what people are saying but also what they are feeling, then many family conversations will become family confrontations.

Most family difficulties can be traced to misunderstanding or lack of good communication skills. Thus, the first rule for building family ties is: Try to understand as much as you can about every family situation. If your family members want to understand one another, the family school must teach them to be both good talkers and good listeners. If you are working at these basic communication skills inside the family circle, you will be much better equipped to understand people and problems outside the family.

3

Be a Good Talker

You might think that this second rule for building family ties is easy to follow. People who live in the same house shouldn't have trouble talking to one another. In fact, there are some people who never seem to stop talking. Being a good talker, however, involves more than simply talking to other family members. It also means learning to communicate so that you express your feelings as well as your ideas.

In many relationships, one party is a talker and the other is a listener. Usually the talker doesn't listen much and the listener rarely talks about important issues. As a result, both parties are unable to discuss their feelings when a problem occurs.

In her book, *Intimate Partners,* Maggie Scarf suggests an exercise for couples who are having problems communicating. The couple sets aside one hour each week. For the first half hour, one partner talks about any subject; the other partner must listen without interrupting. The partners then change roles.

This assignment forces husband and wife to be both talkers and listeners. A partner who usually doesn't express many ideas or emotions often finds it difficult to talk for even that short period of time.

It is not enough, however, to increase the amount of time you spend talking to other family members. The things you talk about and the way you express yourself must convey your desire to improve family relationships. A good talker develops a straightforward style of communicating which helps the listener understand.

You probably know someone like Tom. Ramrod straight, almost to the point of being brittle, Tom's body language conveys a message quite different from his spoken words. He also has definite theories about relationships. When he was dating Mary, he would talk for hours about the importance of commitment, communication, and intimacy. Yet Tom himself has great difficulty trusting other people, and as a result, he never moves beyond the theory. Eventually, Mary, like all his previous girlfriends, realized that Tom's fear of intimacy wouldn't allow him to make a commitment. Her comment was: "I should have recognized his need to control. Anyone that tense obviously isn't going to open up to someone else."

In *Peoplemaking,* family therapist Virginia Satir describes how to be a straightforward communicator. When you are talking, your words, your feelings, and your body must be in harmony. To achieve this harmony, you must know how you *really* feel. Then, you must express these true feelings through words, tone of voice, and body language. Honesty in communication doesn't require that you vent every feeling you have. Rather, it demands that what you say with words and body language be consistent with your feelings. If these things are "in sync" when you communicate, then people will know that your are being honest and straightforward.

To be successful as a spouse and a parent, you must work at being a good talker, a straightforward communicator. If you do, you will create a favorable atmosphere for building family ties.

4

Be an Active Listener

Sarah was busy fixing dinner when a very unhappy, slightly overweight, ten year old Adam burst into the kitchen. Their conversation:

Adam: (whining, but with tears in his eyes) Mommy, Joey said I should go to the "fat kids" farm this summer for my vacation. Sarah: (without looking up) Adam, you're always complaining about something. Why don't you just stay away from Joey if he teases you?

Sarah is a poor listener. She hears Adam's whining but not his hurt feelings. If Sarah makes a habit of being a poor listener, Adam probably expects this response when he cries. Since he learns how to communicate from observing his mother, chances are he, too, is a poor listener. If Sarah were an *active* listener, she would have responded to Adam positively.

Every family has similar communication problems. Given the inevitable bustle of family life, good, active listening is not an automatic response on every occasion.

Everyone has trouble listening—really listening—to what another person is saying. Often, you find yourself wanting to interrupt to make your point. Or, when distracted, you don't pay attention to anything other than the words themselves. Or you think you know exactly what the other person is going to say. Or you imagine the other person doesn't really understand the matter being discussed. As a result, you are frequently a poor listener.

You should therefore listen carefully to the communication experts who emphasize that active listening leads to successful communication. It is also extremely important for building good family ties. To be an active listener you must: 1) give the other person an opportunity to express ideas and feelings—without interrupting; 2) make an honest attempt to understand these ideas and feelings; 3) set aside preconceived opinions about the other person; 4) show respect for the other person's right to hold a view different from yours; 5) demonstrate your appreciation of the effort the other person is making.

If Sarah were an active listener, she would not have attacked Adam for his complaining. Instead, she would have responded to the self-doubts of her overweight child. If she were too busy to give Adam her attention, she would have set a specific time later on to talk about

Joey's teasing. She would then have addressed Adam's concerns about his weight.

You might think that some people are born with the natural ability to be active listeners. More likely, they learned the skill in their family school and work hard at maintaining it. You, too, can be an active listener if you work hard and are willing to unlearn bad communication habits you've picked up. Increased understanding and improved communication in the family will make the effort worth it. As a skilled talker and listener, you'll be able to follow the other rules for making your family work.

5

Be Positive

A father, hearing his wife chastise their two year old, insisted, "Don't call him a bad boy. He'll think he's bad. Call him a good boy and he'll grow up to be good." You might think this father is naive or too permissive. How can just calling a child *good* make him grow up to be good?

Yet the father is wise to follow the advice in the old tune and "accentuate the positive; eliminate the negative." The more you follow this suggestion when dealing with family issues, the greater the chances your family will work. A positive attitude goes a long way toward building good family ties.

Try this useful tool for drawing a favorable picture of your family: make lists of the *pros* and—for this exercise—ignore the *cons*. Even if you already feel positive about your family, you'll probably find it helpful to see your family's best characteristics written out in black and white. You'll be surprised at the traits you've overlooked or taken for granted. If you feel pessimistic about your family, this exercise might help you discover strengths you hadn't been able to see before.

List the good qualities of each family member. Make a list for each member of your immediate family (and extended family if they are regular visitors to your home). Include yourself on the list. Note the positive personality traits, talents, values, attitudes, and achievements of each person.

List positive features in your relationship with each family member. Again, list each family member separately. Note what you give to your relationship with each person. Record what the other person gives to you as well. Do you share interests (work, hobbies, recreational activities, volunteer projects, etc.)? Do you support each other? Do you have good conversations—talking and listening—with this person? What else makes you feel positive when you are with this person?

These lists should give you an overview of your family's many good qualities. Equipped with this understanding, you will be in an excellent position to be positive when you communicate with your family.

Even if you must discuss problems in the family, you'll have much greater success if you accentuate the positive. Instead of beginning a discussion on a critical note, begin by complimenting those involved. Because you've made lists of each person's good traits, your compliments will be sincere and hard to resist. They'll also set the stage for openness to your other comments, which might be more critical.

Communicating positively also means being open to another's understanding of an issue. When you must criticize your spouse or your children, remember there could be positive sides to an issue that you consider a problem. Also, be open to the possibility you have misinterpreted remarks or actions of other family members.

This rule for building good family ties does not mean you should be a *pollyanna*. Rather, it should help you remain hopeful about the possibility that your family can work, even when it is experiencing problems.

6

Respect Others

Donna worries about her teenage and college children. She fears they'll get involved with drugs or expose themselves to AIDS or meet with some other disaster. Donna spies on her children to protect them from these dangers. She searches their rooms for drugs, condoms and birth control pills. Sometimes she steams open their mail before they return home from school or work.

She defends her actions, claiming she has averted problems because of information uncovered in her searches. She wonders why her children don't thank her for protecting them.

Donna's spying is just one example of how little she respects her children. She constantly belittles them in public and compares them with one another. She doesn't stop to think before she talks, and she doesn't bother listening to anyone else's point of view. Her husband doesn't fare any better than his children when Donna sets out to control his life.

Donna doesn't understand the importance of respecting other family members. She lacks a vital skill for building family ties.

You respect another family member when you acknowledge that he or she has the right to make choices. Even when you disagree with a decision, you respect the other person's right to decide. Obviously, you must consider the person's age and emotional maturity when you recognize this right. You're not respecting a two year old if you let the child's temper tantrums dictate the family's social life. As the child grows older, however, parents must recognize his or her need for increased self-determination.

Parents often have difficulty following this rule for building family ties. You are not unusual if you find it difficult to give up control over your child. You probably find it hard to adjust as your children grow up and want to make their own decisions.

Understanding the different stages in your children's lives helps you recognize when they are ready to choose for themselves. The preschooler gets to play with other children on the block. The ten year old can choose not to be in Little League. The high school senior decides whether college is the right choice. The young adult picks a career, a spouse, and a place to live. If you learn to respect your child, you rejoice at each sign of growth, even as you hope the choices will bring success and happiness.

This rule also places demands on husbands and wives. Before marriage, you fantasize about how your spouse will behave after the wedding. The problem with this fantasy is that you create all the situations and all the outcomes. Then, when you're married, your spouse doesn't always follow the script as you've imagined it. He or she acts contrary to your expectations, and you are disappointed. You realize that in real life you lack the control you had in your fantasy world. You then must begin the work of adjusting to your mate as a real person. You must respect your spouse's right to make choices.

When family members respect each person's right to make decisions, a major obstacle to forming good family ties evaporates.

7

Be a Creative Fighter

A group of office workers were discussing marital problems during a coffee break. One older woman, a widow, announced smugly, "Harry and I never had a fight in our twenty-eight years of marriage." When she left the group, a younger woman observed, "Must have been a dull marriage. If you don't fight, you never have the fun of making up." Another commented, "I wonder about people who say they never fight. They must bury a lot of angry feelings. I don't see how two people can live together and not find things they don't agree on." A young bride-to-be in the group said, "I certainly hope Bob and I don't fight when we get married. I can't stand it when people fight."

Fighting means different things to different people. To some people, fighting is a sign of a distressing flaw in a relationship. To others, it implies a healthy discussion of differences. To still others, it suggests overwhelming hostility.

Closely linked with ideas about fighting are ideas about styles of fighting. Sam and Rhonda openly disagree about thirty times a day, no matter who they're with or where they are. Jane and Alex quarrel seldom and only in private but then they bring up every unpleasant event of the previous ten years. Alice and Tom have violent, name-calling, shouting matches when they've had too much to drink.

Usually, your feelings about fighting come from family experiences with fighting. If you agree with the bride-to-be, your children's constant squabbling probably upsets you. So do disagreements with your spouse. If, on the other hand, you are like Sam and Rhonda, arguing is a way of life in your house. It doesn't, however, solve problems.

No matter how you feel about fighting or how your family fights, you should ask yourself if the fighting in your family is productive. Most family fighting is non-productive, that is, people fight, disagree, squabble, and yell about the same things over and over again. They never resolve the issues that provoke conflict in the family.

To make your family work, you must learn to be a creative fighter. You must understand that some family problems won't go away without a confrontation. As a creative fighter, you are not out to destroy others or to win points. Rather, you use confrontation to resolve issues and to move on to a better understanding of other family members.

To be a creative fighter, you must admit that you and others have a right to be angry and express that anger. At the same time, you must be open to the possibility that you don't understand the circumstances that provoke your anger. You need to communicate your feelings as well as your desire to understand and eventually clear up the source of disagreement.

Every family faces conflicts on a regular basis. If your family is to work, you must deal with these conflicts skillfully. Creative fighters respect each other and therefore resolve more conflicts. When you use good communication skills to clear up family disagreements, your creative fighting will lead to better family ties.

8
Be a TLCer

Among a collection of sayings on the family, one seems particularly appropriate to building family ties: ''Family is comfort in grief and joy in time spent together.'' This saying captures why a family can work despite inevitable problems. It also suggests steps family members can take to help build good family ties.

When heartache strikes, nothing works as well as Tender Loving Care (TLC). Life's biggest disappointments lose some of their sting when someone cares. In families that work, family members are attuned to times of grief in one another's lives. They know a little bit of TLC goes a long way to relieve sadness or anxiety.

Consider the story of a teenage girl who arrived at school to learn she had lost the election for student body president. In her heart, she knew she would have been good in the role. Her letdown was greater because the winner was more popular but not as well qualified. Stealing away to a public phone, she called her mother. Immediately sensing her daughter's frustration, the mother said, "It's *their* loss, dear. You would have been a *great* president."

Suddenly, the young woman felt uplifted. Her mother's response was the dose of TLC she needed to feel good about herself again. She felt better equipped to face her fellow students. She knew there would be many more disappointments in life, but—at that moment—she needed her mother's comforting words. And her mother sensed how important it was to support her daughter. If the daughter's disappointment had been completely unrealistic, then the mother may have acted differently. In this case, however, the mother acted as a good TLCer.

Whenever tragedy, loss, disappointment, or illness strikes, family members have an opportunity to help disheartened relatives. A sure way to cement family ties is to be ready to help when your family members need comfort.

It's not always easy to be a TLCer in your family. Daily family life can be full of frustrations and tensions that make it difficult for you to care for other family members' needs. Or the pressures of work might limit your interest in their problems. Or your own unmet needs might cause you to fail to notice others' problems.

Still, with a little effort, you can develop the sensitivity of a TLCer. As a TLCer, you: 1) realize people in trouble can't always articulate their need for comfort; 2) put yourself out to express care and concern to a grieving person; 3) offer assistance when you are able to do so.

The teenage boy who doesn't make the football team becomes a grouch at home. He can't admit his grief. As a TLCer, you recognize why he's being crabby. You serve his favorite meal or invite him to the movies. Later, you give the boy a chance to discuss his feelings. At that time, you help him see he can't take his frustrations out on everyone in the family. By then, your TLC has eased his sorrow and made him more willing to listen.

The ability of family members to give and receive comfort is a sign of good family ties. If your family has difficulty being supportive, work to master the skills of a TLCer. If your family is a comforting one, treasure and care for this ability.

9

Celebration Time

Every family should have a theme song. One family has Kool and the Gang's rendition of "Celebration" as its favorite song. At all big family events—weddings, birthdays, anniversaries—family members take to the dance floor and revel in the rhythm of "a celebration to last throughout the year."

One touching moment in the history of this family and its song took place three months after the father's lung cancer surgery. During a father-daughter dance at the girls' high school, the father and his two teenage daughters teased and laughed as they moved to the rhythm of the song. Mothers, helping with the dance arrangements, stood on the sidelines with tears in their eyes.

More than five years and two operations later, the

father, two daughters, and other family members danced to the song at a son's wedding. For these people, celebration—"joy in time spent together"—is an expression of hope. This family, like every family, has its problems with relationships. Yet celebrating together helps these family members strengthen bonds. Obviously, their brush with death leads them to treasure good times together.

Every family needs celebration time. Celebrating with others means you want to share their happiness. Inviting others to celebrate with you means you want to share your happiness with them. Shared happiness cements family ties that are often strained by problems.

Not everyone comes to family celebrations in a joyful mood. Some participate out of a sense of obligation. Others come with heavy hearts because of their own problems. Still, the atmosphere of celebration encourages openness, helps heal rifts, and provides hope for better relations.

You can nourish the family ties skill of celebrating by actually celebrating and enjoying time spent together. You don't have to search far for a reason to gather the folks together and have a good time. Birthdays, engagements, weddings, anniversaries (and not just of weddings), a new house, a new baby, and holidays (religious and secular) are all opportunities to have family celebrations. So, too, are a new job, a promotion, a raise, school honors, graduations, sports events, and recovery from an illness.

A family gala doesn't have to be an extravaganza. When children are young, doing anything out of the ordinary is a special event. Your desire to commemorate these events as a family makes a lasting impression on them.

Children raised in a happy environment grow up able to find reasons to rejoice with family and friends. The spirit of celebration cultivated in your family will continue as your children celebrate with their children.

Celebrations are a sign of hope. You might not have this in mind when you order the cake or choose the wine. But your decision to celebrate—amidst everyday hassles and world crises—is a sign you still think good will win over evil. Celebrating together builds family hopefulness. Try it. You'll be glad you did.

10

Apologize, Forgive and Forget

Erich Segal's 1970 bestseller, *Love Story*, contains the famous line, "Love means never having to say you're sorry." While this definition sounds very romantic, its impact on building family ties could be disastrous. Saying you're sorry and accepting apologies are crucial skills for good family relationships.

Actually, Segal's line is a cop-out, perhaps typical of the mood of the late 1960's and early 1970's. A more appropriate line would be: *Love means learning to say I'm sorry and meaning it.*

Many families practice the words of the old song, "You Always Hurt The One You Love." Parents, children, and brothers and sisters have strong emotional attachments. As a result, they have many opportunities to hurt and reject one another.

Although you belong to a family, you want to be an individual. You expect family members to understand your needs. You want recognition, respect, acceptance, love, and freedom.

Sometimes your desires clash. On the one hand, you want to grow closer to your spouse and children. On the other hand, you long for the freedom to make your own decisions. These personal decisions sometimes seem to interfere with your desire to grow close to your family. At times, you are aware of the negative impact of your behavior on some individual family member or on the whole family. If you have too much to drink and miss a family party, you know you need to make amends. If you lose your temper with your child because of a fight with your spouse, you know you owe the child an apology. If you had a bad day at the office and take it out on your spouse, you know you're acting unfairly.

At other times, you are thoughtless without realizing it. You aren't paying attention at breakfast when your son asks for help on a school project that evening. You work late and come home to find him in tears. You forget your wife's request that you pick up dessert for the dinner party. You feel tired and you don't recognize your spouse's romantic mood.

In all these instances, you must apologize. If you want your apology to help build family ties, you must also include a sincere promise to try to avoid the unacceptable behavior in the future.

Love means more than saying you're sorry and meaning it, however. Love also means being able to forgive and forget. Unless family members are skilled at accepting apologies and getting on with life, all the other rules for family relationships will prove worthless.

It is legitimate to feel anger or sadness when another family member hurts you. However, prolonged anger and an unwillingness to forgive damage family ties. If, for example, you refuse to accept a legitimate apology from your spouse, your child, or your brother or sister, then the strain in your relationship affects your entire family.

A more deadly attack on family relationships occurs when one family member forgives but won't forget. If you forgive people but constantly bring up their offenses, you lack an essential family ties skill.

Learn to apologize, to forgive, and to forget. You'll then have the skills to create good, loving family ties.

11

Give and Receive

Depending on who is telling the story, Angie is either a martyr or a saint. She does everything for her family without asking anything in return. She cleans the whole house and keeps it immaculate all week. She even cleans her teenagers' rooms. She's a first-rate cook, fixing a hot breakfast every morning and a full-course dinner every evening. She fills everyone's lunch box, putting little notes in each one. She also wears outdated clothes so her children can have the latest fashions.

Angie is a giver. Her husband and children pay a heavy price for Angie's sacrificing nature.

Judy is the exact opposite of Angie. She expects everyone in the family to wait on her. Judy's parents gave her everything she wanted, and she expects her husband and children to do the same. She rarely notices her children's needs, but they must anticipate her every wish. Her husband knows his salary will never satisfy her.

Judy is a taker. Her husband and children also pay a heavy price for her attitude.

Both Angie and Judy lack essential family ties skills. Angie isn't open to receiving anything from other family members. Judy isn't open to giving.

Angie controls people's behavior by giving, giving, giving and supposedly expecting nothing in return. Actually, she expects her family's undying gratitude. By always giving and never letting others give to her, she doesn't allow her husband and children to be contributing members of the family.

Judy's husband and children give a lot to their family. Judy is so self-centered that she contributes little or nothing. She weakens family ties by her insensitivity to the needs of others.

A fundamental principle of family relationships is that you must be both a giver and a receiver. When one person only gives or when one person only takes, the family gets knocked off balance. Resentments are bound to occur.

In any close-knit relationship, all members must be on a relatively equal footing. This doesn't mean each member of your family must contribute exactly the same amount of support all the time. Nor does it mean you should punch a clock for time spent on family chores. Rather, it means there should be a general sense that everyone is doing a fair share to contribute to the family's survival.

At any given time, there are likely to be unequal demands on family members. When the children are young, they demand sacrifices from their parents. Some members of the family become more skilled at certain family chores than others. A wife might be a good cook, so she assumes that role. It may demand more time than the heavy household chores her husband takes over. However, life is never completely fair. Unequal demands on family members can be balanced by emotional support and gratitude.

How would you rate yourself on a giver and receiver scale? If you don't do well in one or the other skill, now is the time to change your behavior.

12

Love Yourself and Your Family

John feels embarrassed by his wife and children. He doesn't think his family measures up to other families in the community. Even when his children receive honors in school and in athletics, he isn't happy. He wants them to do better.

Actually, John's wife manages a good-paying job and an active household. John's children are average to above-average students who do well in many extra-curricular activities. The children are anxious about their abilities, however. They rarely compliment each other on achievements.

John's wife and children feel like they are on a merry-go-round. They struggle to please him, but nothing they do satisfies him. What they don't realize is that John has a very poor image of himself. He wants his family to excel as a way of proving his own worth. His lack of self-love places unreasonable demands on other family members. As a result, no one in John's family has much family pride.

Family pride is the glue that holds a family together. Family pride stirs family members to support one another in times of crisis. When you're proud of your family, you're willing to work on building family ties.

At times, you probably compare your family unfavorably with others, especially when the family is in a down period. If you find you have little, if any, pride in your family, you should examine the reasons for your feelings.

It may be that you don't feel good about yourself, that you have a poor self-image. You will never have any family pride if you aren't proud of yourself. Some people think self-satisfaction and self-love are shameful. These people often admire a false sense of humility that masks a hidden desire for attention.

Real humility, a good quality, comes from an appreciation of your own goodness and the satisfaction that you are doing things to the best of your ability. Pride in the goodness of your family is a natural outgrowth of this attitude.

If you have difficulty feeling good about yourself and your family, you must work at changing your feelings. Refer back to the lists you made earlier. Examine the good qualities you listed for yourself. Were you fair in your assessment? Is your own list shorter than everyone else's?

Did you find it difficult to admit your own goodness? Would you say false humility kept you from admitting your good qualities?

Try rewriting your list, being more aware of your own successes. Concentrate on the things you do well and don't compare yourself with others. Start focusing on these qualities rather than your negative attributes.

Now make a new list that includes the good qualities of your family as a whole. Again, concentrate on *your* family. Don't make comparisons. Refer to this list whenever you find yourself feeling negative about your family.

Don't be like John. Become skilled at nurturing self-love and family pride in yourself and in other family members. You've got to love yourself and your family to make your family work.

13

Learn to Laugh

The family called it the Case of the Missing Pens. Bob would bring a pen home; some family member would borrow it—"just for a second"—and it would disappear. It happened over and over again. No matter how many pens Bob brought home, family members could never find one when they needed it.

Bob did a fair amount of complaining about his problem with pens. Fortunately, his family knew he had a sense of humor. No one ever took his complaints too seriously. Everyone, including Bob (though he would never admit it), began to treat the pen problem as a joke. Like the socks that disappear in the dryer, the car keys that are always missing, and the eyeglasses that can't be found, the disappearing pens became a family mystery and a family joke.

For Bob's fiftieth birthday, his daughter bought fifty pens. She wrote "Happy Birthday" on fifty pieces of paper and attached one to each pen. She placed the pens in various spots where Bob would be sure to find them. Bob's pen problem moved from family joke to family legend.

Of course, less than two months later, there wasn't a pen to be found. Bob was free to complain again.

Obviously, many family problems are much more serious than that of the missing pens. Yet the tensions can be relieved when people are willing to see the humorous side of even the most serious situation.

A husband and wife were in the midst of a bitter quarrel. It was about a problem to which there was no solution. Nonetheless, each was set on winning a losing battle. If the quarrel had continued, their marriage would have been severely strained. In the midst of a screaming match, however, their two year old broke the tension by modeling his mother's high-heeled shoes. His parents couldn't help but laugh at his antics. Once they let down their guard, they saw the foolishness of their argument.

Laughter and good humor don't ridicule. Bill Cosby pokes fun at some important problems in a growing family, but people laugh because he captures the flaw of taking life too seriously.

Some people see family life as serious business. The premise of this book is that it takes hard work to make a family work. Yet hard work does not have to be unpleasant and forbidding. Your burden can be lighter—and your task more rewarding—if you learn to laugh.

You delude yourself if you think you can make your family perfect. It's precisely this illusion of perfection that gets shattered in a Cosby routine. While you laugh at him, he allows you the freedom to laugh at yourself. You come away knowing you still have to work at building family ties. You also know that no matter how hard you work, you will always be tripped up by human imperfection.

Cultivate humor and laughter in your family and you will make the work of building family ties bearable. If you trip, humor will soften the fall. You can then approach seemingly insolvable family problems with the old cliche, "If I don't laugh, I'll cry."

14

Don't Triangle

Marilyn and Richard have a troubled marriage. Richard is a workaholic. Marilyn doesn't like confrontation. Instead, she stews in private about his work habits. She wonders at times if he is seeing other women.

Marilyn turns to her children for support. She tells them how their father neglects the family by his long working hours. She hints that he might be unfaithful. Gene, a teenager, is hostile toward his father. He takes his mother's side whenever a disagreement flares into a bitter fight.

In fact, Richard has felt left out of his family circle for a long time. He buries himself in his work because he feels useless around his family. The only time he feels worthwhile is when his teenage daughter acts up. Then, he and Marilyn must unite against the child.

The Allen family is a classic example of unhealthy family relationships. Psychologists call this pattern "triangling." It is not at all unusual for parents to relate to each other through a child, thus forming a triangle. This solution to a marital rift allows the parents to avoid their own relationship problems.

Triangles occur as a way of de-escalating tensions in many relationships. They can help defuse a situation that might otherwise lead to a breakdown in communication. In families, however, triangles become ingrained and destroy all hope of good family ties.

Three different triangle patterns occur in families:

1. A secret alliance forms between one parent and a child. They work together to undermine the authority of the other parent.

2. One parent, most often the father, withdraws from the strain in the marriage and leaves the mother to focus her frustration on the child.

3. Parents unite on only one issue—the problems created by a "difficult" child.

If you are serious about making your family work, avoid triangles at all costs. To avoid forming triangles in your family, abide by the following:

1. Refuse to take sides in any family confrontation.

2. Don't voice or listen to negative complaints about a third party.

3. Don't try to make your children assume a role that belongs to your spouse.

4. Don't let problems with your children become an excuse for not dealing with serious issues in your marriage.

Triangling sets a bad example for children. They grow up without learning other ways of relating. In their adult relationships they continue this practice of triangling. Continuing problems with in-laws could mean a couple is avoiding problems in their own marriage.

Healthy family ties and triangling cannot exist in the same family. Become skilled at stopping this practice whenever it occurs.

15
Don't Blame

Stan and Betty fight about anything and everything. They each blame the other for the troubles in their marriage. Stan and Betty are violators of a basic rule of communication: they are blamers.

The pattern of their fighting is always the same. Betty complains about something Stan does, such as leaving his dirty clothes on the floor. Stan responds angrily to her complaint. He then blames all the troubles in his life on Betty's complaining. Betty continues complaining and blames Stan for not helping enough around the house. From that point on, the fighting disintegrates into a blaming contest. Both try to outdo each other in assigning blame for their difficulties.

Betty and Stan are experts at blaming. After a while, it's obvious they are blaming each other for more than the objection that started the fight. Betty blames Stan for not being the person she thought she was marrying. Stan blames Betty for failing to live up to his dream of a perfect wife.

As long as they are busy blaming each other for specific bad habits, neither Betty nor Stan needs to look at this deeper cause of their unhappiness. Nor do they need to work at understanding why they are unhappy. Consequently, they don't have to work at eliminating the reasons for their discontent.

Blaming others is a guaranteed way to destroy family communication. When you accuse another person, you shift the focus from your own inability to deal with disappointment. *You* don't have to change. The other person does. If Stan began picking up his dirty clothes and helping around the house, Betty would likely find another reason to complain.

When people get married, they expect their spouse to solve all their problems. The inevitable complications of family life shatter this fantasy. Before marriage, you imagine your future partner will do away with whatever pain you suffered in previous family relationships. When you find your relationship with your spouse has its own difficulties, you have two choices: you either recognize how unrealistic your expectations were or you blame your spouse for your unhappiness.

Since no one is perfect, your spouse is bound to do things that irritate you. You will have many legitimate complaints during the lifetime of a marriage. However, you can't blame your spouse for your expectation that marriage and family life would be perfect. As long as you refuse to accept responsibility for your disappointment, you will use legitimate complaints to blame your spouse for your shattered dreams.

If you want to stop being a blamer, you must assume your share of responsibility for your marital problems. You must recognize that you will only achieve the dream of a happy marriage when you and your spouse are willing to work at developing relationship skills.

16

Don't Manipulate

Marie is a sickly woman. When her children were young, they couldn't do anything that might upset their mother and cause another sick spell. Her husband couldn't accept a promotion because Marie wasn't strong enough to make the move to another city.

Now that her children are older, they notice a pattern to their mother's illness. As long as everyone in the family does what Marie wants, she has no health problems. As soon as someone even hints at disagreeing with her plans, Marie takes to her bed. Everyone worries about her health and the dissenter gives up the cause. With things going her way again, Marie gets better.

She is a manipulator. Manipulators are very poor at relationships. They are unable to admit to problems and then work to make changes. Instead, they control other peoples' behavior through devious means. Manipulators perform emotional blackmail, threatening disaster if their wishes aren't met.

Everyone manipulates from time to time. Sometimes, it takes too much effort to admit to yourself and explain to the other person why you want them to do your bidding. Instead, you try to guilt your child into behaving. Or you withhold affection from your spouse. Or you sulk when your parent gives you a curfew. None of these behaviors help build good family ties.

When manipulating becomes a pattern in a family, the ties that bind members together may be strong, but they are unhealthy. No one learns how to deal with real feelings or admit real desires. Underneath a surface harmony, frustration builds. Eventually, the frustration explodes in angry outbursts that further erode family ties.

Often, one family member is a skilled manipulator. The comic strip *Momma* pokes fun at a parent who tries to control her adult children. Momma Hobbes' three children are a disappointment. One son married a woman his mother considers inferior. Another son is an unemployed young adult who dates beautiful woman when he should be taking care of Momma. Instead of dating the professional men her mother considers good husband material, her daughter brings home an assortment of the losers of the world. In this comic world, Momma's manipulation always fails.

Unfortunately, in real life, Momma and Poppa's manipulation works. Parents, too, can be targets of manipulation by their children. Teenagers, young adults, and even older adults often try to make parents feel guilty for the mistakes they made when their children were young.

Be aware of the times you use guilt, sickness or withholding of love to achieve your wishes. Also be alert to the times others use these devices to control you. Stop any of your manipulative behavior. Resist all attempts by others to manipulate you. Instead, foster honesty in family communications so no one feels he or she has to resort to manipulation to achieve a goal.

If you want good family ties, you must work to rid your family of manipulative relationships.

17

Seek Outside Help

The Bailey family is extremely troubled. Ed Bailey is an alcoholic who won't admit he has a problem. His daughter, Susan, is anorexic. His wife, Sandy, has trouble sleeping.

In any given week, the Baileys break all the rules for good family relationships. Even if they knew about family ties skills, the Baileys wouldn't be able to practice them. Their energy is drained by deep emotional problems.

Obviously, the Baileys need outside help to solve their individual and family problems. Sandy knows she must join a self-help group or get professional counselling if she is to help Ed and Susan. She also knows that Ed and Susan need outside help. Whether any of them will seek this help is uncertain. Still, it's apparent to everyone outside the family that they need help.

Families like the Baileys are not the only ones needing outside help with family problems. Often, a family can't practice family ties skills unless an individual member or the entire family gives up a harmful way of behaving. In some instances, people want to develop a skill but aren't able to master it on their own.

A person who has been a poor talker or a poor listener all his or her life might not be able to recognize or change this shortcoming without some help in communication skills. A manipulator's behavior might be so extreme that only a professional would be able to discourage it. A martyr's children might be so frustrated by their parent's behavior that they become rebellious and need professional help. The marriage of a taker could become so bad that, without professional help, there would be no hope of saving it.

Unfortunately, many other serious family problems are not as obvious as those in the Bailey family. Regardless of its nature, if any emotional problem prevents family members from developing family ties skills, that's a sure sign outside assistance (professional advice or self-help groups) is needed. This is the only way to restore peace in the family. The difficulties, especially if they are hidden, will not go away on their own. The family will remain troubled. Moreover, the family will not be able to work together to ward off problems outside the home.

Yet many families tolerate a high degree of turmoil rather than seek professional help. Advice columnists repeatedly urge troubled readers to "get professional counselling." Still, there is a stigma, often self-induced, surrounding the idea of seeking help with your problems. If you are like most people, you feel you ought to be able to solve your problems on your own. Other people seem to manage, and you think you have some shortcoming when you can't. There might be a valid reason why you can't manage in a particular situation, however, and it might be unrelated to anything you ever did. If you are held back by forces you don't understand or can't control, then seeking help is a sign of strength, not weakness.

If no amount of good will and effort helps you and your family master the family ties skills in the previous chapters, then you must practice this final skill.

18

A Family Ties Skills Review

Before exploring how a family survives the stresses and strains of modern life, you should review your family ties skills rating.

First, retake the test in Chapter 1. When you finish the test the second time, consider the following questions:

1) Did you answer any of the questions differently the second time? Would you want to?

2) Why do you think you made the choices you did each time you took the test?

3) Can you suggest alternatives that weren't even mentioned for any of the questions? What made you think of these alternatives?

4) What would you like your score to be on the family ties skills test?

5) What must you do to achieve this score?

6) Do you or does anyone in your family need outside help to overcome obstacles to good family ties?

Next, make a list of which family ties skills your family should foster. Mark them in order of importance. Note what steps you must take to improve your own skills. In addition, note how you might encourage these skills in other family members. If you see the need for outside help, list what contacts you should make.

Finally, review your family ties skills test from time to time. Also review the Dos and Don'ts for building family ties. Follow your progress in improving your skills and making your family work.

Your family will work if you and other family members are willing to make the effort to master these basic family ties skills. The skills help you follow the principles of good relationships in a family setting. Since many of these skills are simply common sense, you might find yourself much better at building family ties than you had first imagined.

Nevertheless, the close-knit environment of family life leads to intense feelings among family members. When these feelings are disruptive, it is difficult for a family to function satisfactorily. In that case, practicing family ties skills can help steer a family back to the right course.

If a family is not good at family ties skills, it will have trouble dealing with the pressures of the larger world beyond the home. Family members who foster good family relationships, however, can work together to cope with the pressures of the 1980's and into the next century.

In short, your family relationships strongly influence how you survive in the world beyond the home. Good family ties nurture the self-confidence needed to cope both in the home and in the larger society. You'll have to work at making your family work, but you'll be rewarded by the comfort and joy that only a family can bring. Don't pass up any opportunity to improve the quality of your family ties.

Part Two:
Stresses, Strains & Strengths

19

Till Death Do Us Part

An excellent proverb mentioned earlier serves as the first lesson in the school for family relationships: Children learn more from what their parents do than from what their parents say. It follows logically that building strong marriage ties teaches your children about relationships. Making your marriage work is an important first step towards making your family work.

Making marriage work in the 1980's might seem like a nearly impossible task. Some social commentators idealize the "good old days" when people stayed together "until death do us part." They decry social conditions that put negative pressures on today's marriages. Still, if you want to build long-term marriage ties, you can find supports for this goal not available in the "good old days."

Some of the very social conditions accused of contributing to the breakup of marriages also help people build strong marriage ties. Longer lives, new possibilities for women, changing male/female roles, and the freedom to choose who you marry and whether to stay married all can cause stress in a marriage. Yet each of these social conditions also offers you opportunities to enrich your married life. If you are in your marriage for the "long haul," you must take advantage of these opportunities.

Two specifics to bear in mind as you build marriage ties: 1) *Acknowledge that all relationships go through cycles.* Don't think your marriage is the only relationship to go through highs and lows. There is a pattern to the marriage cycle that often runs the gamut from ecstasy to despair, sometimes in the course of one day.

First, you fall in love. The "walking on air" feelings of your courtship days feed your daydreams about the joys of married life. You and your beloved wear rose-colored glasses. You are oblivious to flaws in each other and in your relationship. You want to spend the rest of your life exploring the wonders of each other's bodies, minds, and hearts.

Next, as you settle into your marriage, you develop habits in your relationship. The spontaneity of your courtship gives way to routines required for everyday living. You develop some routines consciously: who will pay the bills; who will do the wash. Others evolve without your knowing it: you put the groceries in certain places and your spouse follows suit. Some routines are good: you make an effort to compliment each other on your appearance. Others are dangerous for your relationship: one person always initiates sex; you put off discussing problems.

The unconscious and dangerous routines cause you to take each other for granted. This is the major obstacle to continued growth in your marriage. Without growth, you move into the next stage in the marriage cycle: reaching the pits. Sometimes, a trivial incident—once more, your spouse forgot to pick up the cleaning—will trigger your despair. You wonder what happened to the excitement of your courtship days. At other times, a major disagreement you never anticipated causes you to question your marriage vows.

At these turning points in your marriage, you must decide whether to fight over the problem—and risk the consequences—or whether to remain in the pits. The only other alternative is to end the marriage. Indeed, repeated decisions to remain in the pits usually lead to the divorce court.

A fight need not be an hysterical, name-calling, blaming match. You can be creative fighters, using all the family ties communication skills to move out of the pits. You don't have to continue going around in circles, never resolving your differences. When you conquer one of the untold number of obstacles facing your marriage, you'll begin to hope you can survive other problems.

This new hope gives you the confidence you need to

fall in love all over again. Creative fighting makes falling in love the second, third, hundredth, or thousandth time better than every previous time including the first time.

2) Keep romance alive. The strong physical attraction of your courtship days had much to do with the romance of that time. You never even noticed each other's negative qualities. Your heart beat faster at just the thought of your lover. What difference did it make that you might not always agree on important issues? All that mattered was that you were in love. Your heart and your body told you to risk committing yourself. And you did, with little concern for the consequences.

Throughout your marriage, you must nurture this romantic love with its sexual attraction and nonjudgmental view of your lover. The ups and downs of married life, the realization that the "perfect" mate is only human, and the need for repeated reconciliations put a damper on your early daydreams of marital bliss. Without the balance of romantic love, the work of building marriage ties would be a burdensome chore.

You enhance your marriage as you become better players at the game of sexual intimacy. To be good sexual intimacy players, you must learn the techniques of the game and show respect for your fellow player.

Sexual intimacy is supposed to be playful. Contrary to the Playboy understanding of sexuality, a good playmate (male or female) is not simply an object. In sexual intimacy, you work together, not in competition. Your goal is to share ecstasy with your mate, not just to seek your own pleasure. The sharing of bodies is a fraud unless you commit yourself to a sharing of dreams and hopes.

When you act on this commitment, your marriage bonds become stronger. Your glasses don't need to be rose-colored. Instead, you begin to see exciting new things about your *real* partner, not just the one of your daydreams. In addition, as you become skilled sexual playmates, sharing your bodies, minds, and hearts, you find it easier to be creative fighters. The potential loss of a good sexual playmate leads you to tackle problems before you get too far into the pits.

Keep romance alive through the ups and downs of marriage, and you'll be inspired to make your marriage work. When you and your spouse work at making your marriage work, you are developing a first-rate school for family relationships.

20

The Big One?

A group of experts sat around discussing how people could combat the pits of married life. A psychologist had one suggestion, a sociologist, another. A woman writer added several more. Finally, the clergyman asked, "How do they deal with the Big One?" "The Big One?" they replied in unison. The clergyman said that in his marriage counselling experience an affair was the one problem that had no solution. People couldn't let go of their anger and hurt over a spouse's affair.

The majority of Americans still disapprove of extramarital sex. They believe fidelity is important in marriage even if they aren't faithful themselves. Some experts estimate that almost half the wives and over half the husbands have affairs by their fortieth birthdays. If these estimates are anywhere near accurate, many family ties suffer the Big One's negative effects.

Questions to mull over when making judgments about affairs: Is the affair a symptom of basic incompatibility or a reaction to frustration in the relationship? Is sexual cheating due to an individual's inability to make a lifelong commitment? Is there ever a time when a lapse in fidelity wouldn't harm a marriage? How would you react if your spouse had an affair? Finally, is an affair the *only* Big One?

Consider Kay and Pete. Pete travels regularly. In the twenty years of their marriage, he has had many one-night stands with women business contacts. He says it doesn't harm their marriage as long as Kay is unaware of his philandering. He claims an affair would be different. He never gets involved with a woman on a long-term basis.

Nevertheless, repeated sexual infidelities with many different partners show an inability or an unwillingness to make a commitment. Men and women who engage in one night stands or many short affairs don't build strong marriage bonds. Yet they don't run the risk of involvement with anyone else either.

They are sexually immature, unable to see the connection between their sexual activities and their marital commitment. While they fool themselves that their marriages are O.K., they run a constant risk of discovery. For some, this risk adds to the excitement.

Someone like Pete needs help to uncover the roots of his pattern of unfaithfulness. Actually, Kay and Pete both need help building their marriage bond. Probably the only way they will get help is for Kay to be shattered by a discovery of Pete's unfaithfulness. Even then, it will be hard to overcome the damage of repeated infidelity.

Any discovery of infidelity, be it a long affair, a single indiscretion, or many one night stands, comes as a shock. You might initially be devastated by even a single indiscretion. Yet sometimes you can understand how circumstances tempted your spouse. At times, anyone could be tempted to be unfaithful. If everyone gave into temptation, however, there would be no marital fidelity.

Thus, even one indiscretion is a sign that the marriage bond needs serious attention. If your spouse is sorry and agrees to work on building the marriage ties, your marriage can still survive. But you both will have to work hard at family ties skills.

On the other hand, an affair is a statement about the condition of the marriage. Often, the partner having the affair gives up on the marriage before the affair. The affair then becomes the excuse to end the marriage.

At other times, when communication seems impossible, a spouse may use an affair to highlight a crisis. The affair then becomes a message about the seriousness of the crisis. In a case like this, it might be possible to save your marriage. Still, the task of rebuilding trust in a marriage requires a serious commitment from both partners. If you can work to rebuild trust, you might succeed in improving your marriage. Yet, as the clergyman said, the hurt and anger are great. An affair is a risky way to communicate your unhappiness.

However, an affair isn't the only Big One. Take the case of John and Alice. They have been physically faithful for the twelve years of their marriage. Yet their sex life is dull. They've settled into a routine of "in, out, and roll over" sex, usually on Saturday night. They never discuss their sexual relationship.

In fact, they discuss very little. John comes home from work, has a few drinks, eats dinner, and falls asleep watching TV. Alice comes home from work, fixes dinner, helps the children with homework, does some household chores, gets the children to bed, and collapses around midnight. On weekends, John does some yard work, plays cards with his friends, and watches sporting events. Alice shops for groceries, does the heavy housework, visits her mother, and goes to the shopping mall. Once in a while, on a Saturday night, they go out with friends.

John and Alice's marriage is as much in the pits as any where a spouse is having an affair. They are neglecting their sexual relationship. They aren't playmates for each other. As a result, they have no incentive to get out of their rut. In addition, they aren't good communicators or creative fighters. They are content to drift along, probably both discontent, but unwilling or unable to make a change. Their Big One is indifference.

If this is your situation, you and your spouse are both ripe for an affair. If one of you did have an affair, you probably would blame the affair for the breakup of your marriage. Actually, the culprit would be your indifference to growth in your relationship. Even if neither of you has an affair, you are guilty of unfaithfulness to your vows.

One of you must shatter the indifference. You must initiate communication. If you and your spouse can't work on communication, you need couple or individual counselling.

Your own Big One (the seemingly unsolvable marital problem) might not be like the ones illustrated in these two tales. Whatever your story, if you have a Big One, you are destroying your marriage bonds. If you and your spouse both want to save your marriage, you need to call all the family ties skills into play. If you and your spouse still find it impossible to communicate, your marriage is not likely to survive the strain of the Big One.

21

Severing the Bond

As they left the divorce court, Joe turned to Irene, a smug grin on his face. "Well, your lawyer certainly didn't do you any favors," he said. Irene claims this scene captures the spirit of their whole relationship. Years later, they still haven't moved beyond their anger and hurt at the death of their marriage.

For every divorce, there are many stories of stress and strain. Even the spouse initiating the break feels stressed when divorce becomes the only way out of the marriage pit.

The sharp increase in the divorce rate in the 1970's was followed by a leveling off and slight decline in the 1980's. Even so, many families in the 80's are experiencing the stress of divorce, especially younger families. The National Opinion Research Center's *General Social Surveys* show a forty percent divorce rate for marriages of people born between 1945 and 1960. For people in those broken marriages, building family ties in the future depends on how well they deal with the trauma of divorce.

You hear stories about friendly divorces and read books about creative divorces. The reality is that divorce is a very messy situation. Divorce might be the only solution to a destructive marriage bond but that doesn't mean it's pleasant. Emotionally, you go through a process of grief not unlike what you would feel at the death of a loved one. Financially, you must make adjustments you never anticipated. Socially, you are no longer a member of the couple who socialized with family and friends. To create a new life after your divorce, you must deal with this emotional, financial, and social damage.

Dealing with the emotional damage. Before going on to new relationships, you must give yourself time to grieve over the death of your marriage. Some people, unwilling to admit their grief, immediately become involved in a new relationship. Others enter into a series of short-term relationships. These people usually wind up repeating the same behavior that destroyed their marriages. The gay divorcee and the swinging new bachelor are running away from the trauma of their divorce.

Grieving after your divorce doesn't require a public display of your pain. Rather, it is a process in which you come to terms with your own mixed feelings. Over a period of time, you begin to let go of the hold your broken marriage has on you. You find the emotional energy to rebuild your self-confidence and get on with your life.

Some people find that a self-help group provides needed support for a positive grieving process. Moreover, in a good self-help group, you learn that people do survive the trauma of divorce. Indeed, you find that many people have gone on to lead much happier lives than they led when in the pits of marriage. Be careful, however, of a self-help group where members waste emotional time and energy blaming former spouses for all their problems.

Even as you grieve, you must figure out what went wrong in your marriage. Why weren't you and your spouse able to keep your marriage together? Did you make a wrong choice in the first place? Did you marry to avoid dealing with a family problem only to have the problem reappear in your marriage? Were you expecting too much from your marriage? From your spouse? Could you have done something earlier in your marriage to keep the problem from reaching the proportions it did? If you can't find satisfactory answers to these questions on your own, you should seek out a counselor who has had experience helping people survive divorce.

Dealing with the financial damage. One of the first discoveries you make after a separation is that two can't live as cheaply when they live apart. When it becomes obvious that the divorce will cause a financial strain, money quickly becomes the focus of your disputes. Money problems can continue to plague you years after a divorce. Ten years after her divorce, Irene is still bitter about being cheated by Bob.

In most divorces, the woman suffers the greater financial damage. In *The Divorce Revolution*, Lenore Wietzman presents evidence to show that the average man experiences a financial gain after a divorce, while the average woman suffers a loss. Over the years, his income increases forty-two percent while hers decreases seventy percent. If you are a woman and these averages reflect your situation, you probably are as bitter as Irene.

Don't let money problems continue the upheaval that marked the end of your marriage. Get expert advice about the financial needs and obligations of you and your spouse. Try to work out a fair and reasonable settlement. If necessary, get an unbiased person to help you negotiate a financial arrangement. If you are unable to get a fair settlement, you will have to develop other sources of income. Investigate what governmental aid is available. In addition, consider ways you might increase your own earning power. Otherwise, fighting about money will keep you from building a new life.

Dealing with the social damage. Immediately after a divorce, you may wonder how you will manage socially as a single rather than as part of a couple. Building a new social life after a divorce is crucial for your recovery. You need to regain confidence in your ability to make and keep friends.

Don't fall into the trap of the singles bars. Instead, involve yourself in activities you enjoy. That way you'll meet people with mutual interests. Friendships developed out of common interests can be strong and lasting. When you feel confident in your ability to survive socially as a single, you will be on the way to a new life.

Dealing with the tie that still binds. You must learn to deal with whatever ties you still have to your former mate. Even though you sever the marriage bond, you don't erase all the effects of that marriage from your life. The practice of referring to "my ex" long after a divorce proves that memories of your marriage linger on. You often discover that these memories aren't always all bad.

Children make the tie even stronger and longer. Soon after the last child support payment, there is a wedding. Then, there is a grandchild, yet another sign that the tie continues ever so loosely.

The sooner you work through the emotional, financial, and social damage of a divorce, the sooner you will get on with your life. Then it will be easier to accept this tie without bitterness. You'll also be free to build other ties.

22

What About the Children?

At one time, parents remained in all but the most intolerable marriages "for the sake of the children." Then, experts challenged that theory. They said children were better off in a peaceful home with one parent than in a conflict-ridden home with both parents. Some people concluded you should divorce for the sake of the children.

In extreme cases such as child abuse, violent alcoholism, or mental difficulties, divorce does protect the children from physical harm. In most other cases, what's best for the child is parents who develop family ties skills and work at making their family and marriage work.

However, some spouses can't build marriage ties. Others don't get out of the marriage pits. Still others don't want the responsibility of family ties. So, parents divorce and disrupt their children's lives.

Even if you divorce to protect your children from harm, they will be upset. They, too, experience emotional, financial, and social damage. Their anger and grief are real and legitimate. How you deal with your children's feelings determines how they will survive the damage of divorce.

In an ideal situation, concern for your children would be your top priority. You would prepare the children for the eventual split. You would negotiate a settlement based on the best interest of the children. You would be a responsible parent, even in the midst of a divorce. Unfortunately, when your own turmoil is great, it's difficult to consider your children's needs.

If you have children and are in the process of a divorce, pay attention to their feelings about the divorce. Let your children express their worries and concerns. Examine your reactions to their anger or fear. Then, identify how you might help them come to terms with the family breakup. Be a good listener and a good talker.

If you and your spouse work together to help your children through the divorce, you repair some of the damage the divorce does to the school for family relationships. If, for whatever reason, you and your spouse can't work together, use family ties skills yourself when you are with your children. Eventually, they will benefit from your example.

Some points to remember when dealing with your children:

1. It's your divorce, not your children's. Many parents

go to great lengths to assure the children the divorce is a problem between Mom and Dad. Mom still loves them. Dad still loves them. Mom and Dad just can't love each other anymore. You need to carry this idea to its logical conclusion. Your children had no say in the divorce decision. You are creating an unpleasant situation for them. You can't expect them to accept it without protest.

Maybe you realize divorce is the only way out of a horrible family situation. However, your children don't understand the depth of your problems. All they see is the end of their family. Understandably, they are upset. Respect your child's right to mourn, to be confused, to be angry, to be hurt, to be worried about the future.

2. The age of the child plays a big part in the reaction to the parents' divorce. If you have more than one child, don't expect them all to react the same way. Preschoolers might think they have driven the absent parent away. A six or seven year old is apt to feel sadness, fear, and panic. A preteen who sees things as either black or white will want to blame one parent. Teenagers might see the necessity for the divorce yet be angry at this added disruption to their teen years.

3. Never ask a child to take sides. Even if you didn't triangle with your child against your spouse before the divorce, you will be tempted to do so now. It takes great restraint to avoid asking your child to side with you in disputes with your ex-spouse. Be conscious of the subtle ways in which you play on your child's desire to support you.

Barbara's preteen daughter, Beth, is furious with her father for deserting the family for another woman. Barbara is angry, too. Still she restrains her anger around Beth. Although she would like her daughter's support, she knows the girl also needs to respect and love her father. She tries to help Beth see that her father doesn't bear all the blame for the breakup of the marriage. Though this is difficult for Barbara, she is giving Beth the opportunity to work out her feelings towards her father.

4. Your children need a sounding board for their feelings. Louise complains because her pre-teen and teenage children never talk about the divorce. The children tell a friend they don't want to be disloyal to their parents. They keep their feelings to themselves because they don't want to say anything bad about either parent.

A good support for children comes from other children going through the same experience. With the guidance of a qualified adult, self-help groups give children an opportunity to discuss their feelings with their peers. Often, peer suggestions are easier to take than those of adults. Children who've participated in these groups say it has helped to know they're not alone.

5. Experts claim it takes about three years for most children to come to terms with their parents' divorce. When you work on family ties skills with your children, you help them bounce back from the shock of divorce. Practicing family ties skills will help them overcome the bad effects of the divorce.

If your child doesn't bounce back, shows signs of great

immaturity, or engages in disruptive behavior, you should seek professional help. Some children can't adjust on their own and need professional guidance.

6. All children have problems from time to time. Whenever one of her children has a problem, Marion wonders if it is because of her divorce. Her worry causes Marion to feel guilty and encourages the children to manipulate her. If you fall into this trap with your children, they will grow up breaking an important family ties rule.

7. Finally, don't be afraid to ask for advice on how to help your children. If you are not a child of divorce yourself, you don't know what they are feeling. Read about children and divorce. Ask other parents about their experiences. If necessary, talk to an expert. You can't stop working at making your family work after a divorce. In fact, for a while, you will have to work even harder.

23

Separated Parenting

Margaret has custody of her daughter and two sons. Margaret always dreamt her children would grow up in a secure family. She wanted them to enjoy all the advantages of middle-class suburbia. She would stay home with them.

Divorce shattered her dream. Henry, who remarried soon after the divorce, provides for the children's financial well being. He doesn't think they need suburban advantages, however. Margaret had to resume working to provide for her own financial future and for extras for her children.

She feels guilty because the failure of her marriage robbed her children of the dream. So, Margaret rushes from work to the dancing lessons of one child, the tennis match of another child, and the baseball game of the third child. She also does parent-teacher conferences, grocery shopping, and the many other parenting duties that are shared in a two-parent family.

In addition, she is the authority figure for her children. She deals with all their disputes. She decides the appropriate punishment for misbehavior. She sets the limits for her teenagers. She worries when they are out late on a Saturday night. On the periodic Friday evening when Henry takes the children out for dinner, Margaret collapses. She is exhausted. Parenting is never easy. Parenting on your own is more than twice as hard.

In nine out of ten divorces when the father does not contest it, the mother receives *sole custody* of the children. She has legal and physical responsibility for them. The father has visiting rights. Fathers who have chosen to fight for custody of their children have been successful sixty-four percent of the time. As the movie *Kramer vs. Kramer* shows, a father with custody also has his set of problems.

Other custody arrangements include:

Split custody - the father takes one or more child and the mother does the same. This plan splits the children from brothers and sisters as well as from the absent parent, breaking the family apart even more.

Divided custody - each parent takes the children for part of the year and is responsible for them during that time. This arrangement relieves each parent of the sole responsibility for the child, but does not require cooperation between the parents.

Joint custody - the parents share legal responsibility for the children and usually share physical custody as well. Both parents remain *actively* involved in their children's lives. The children might live four days a week in one home and three in another. Or they might alternate weeks. For this option to succeed, the parents must communicate well and have the ability to cooperate and compromise. Divorce experts see only about ten percent of divorced couples who demonstrate these skills. Still, they consider this the best custody plan.

Whatever custody arrangement you settle on, it will be successful for building family ties only if you and your ex-mate work at making it work. If you are the only parent concerned about family ties, you still can follow certain practices that will encourage these skills in your children.

As *the custodial parent,* you should: 1. be realistic in your demands on yourself, recognizing you can't be a superparent; 2. work with your children to determine what's necessary for a well-run house and a reasonably happy family life; 3. discuss with your children the limitation on your time and energy; 4. avoid blaming the divorce for every time and financial shortage; 5. be consistent in your discipline but, as children grow older, be open to discussing possible changes in rules; 6. encourage your child to stay in touch with the other parent; 7. find support people (babysitters, relatives, friends) who will provide you with free time; 8. use your free time doing things you enjoy so you'll be a happier person around your children.

As *the non-custodial parent,* you should: 1. develop common interests with your children; 2. avoid forcing your children to spend their time with you doing things they don't enjoy; 3. resist always doing things with them you don't enjoy, thus making the visits a burden; 4. be dependable and punctual, remembering how important a promise is to a child; 5. refrain from trying to buy affection; 6. realize your child will sometimes prefer spending time with a friend or participating in a sporting event instead of being with you.

Both parents should: 1. abstain from putting each other down; 2. avoid direct contradiction of the other parent's directive—unless it is life- threatening; 3. resist using the child to communicate your anger and hostility to your ex-spouse; 4. listen to the child's concerns about problems with the custody arrangement; 5. hold back from quizzing your child about the other parent's lifestyle; 6. resist prying into the child's relationship with the other parent; 7. refrain from making the child feel guilty when you are left alone; 8. refuse to compete with the other parent for the child's affection; 9. make sure your child stays in touch with grandparents, aunts, uncles, cousins; 10. be prepared for your child to be hesitant about your romantic involvements; 11. be aware that your children's feelings and interests will change, as will their satisfaction with the custody plan; 12. consider counselling, individual or family (including the other parent), if there are problems.

You, your ex-spouse, and your children must adjust your expectations about parenting. Separated parenting requires hard work if it is to work well. You'll find family ties skills even more important as you try to support your children through their growing years.

24

Stepping

Gretchen, a widow with two teenage daughters, is dating Ron, the custodial father of a teenage daughter and two preteen sons. Ron's alcoholic wife has remarried twice since divorcing Ron when the youngest child was three years old.

Gretchen has very definite ideas about childrearing. She is a strict disciplinarian and doesn't believe in spoiling her children just because they are fatherless. She teaches them to be responsible young women.

For the eight years since his divorce, Ron has given in to his children's every whim. A successful businessman, he tries to make up for their loss of a mother by showering his children with possessions. The children are demanding of Ron and ill-mannered and discourteous around Gretchen.

Gretchen loves Ron. Yet she turns down his monthly marriage proposals. "It'd never work," she says. "I know of too many second marriages ruined by kids. I'd go crazy trying to be the mother in that house. And my daughters would clash with his children."

Family life observers agree that building family ties in a stepfamily is the hardest relationship task they come across. Being successful as a stepparent takes advanced family ties skills. Although every stepmother isn't like Cinderella's and all sisters don't pick on their stepsisters, adding new people into a parent-child relationship is difficult.

And yet, many single parents look to remarriage as the solution to problems with family life. In the 1980's, most divorced men and many divorced women are remarrying. In the United States, there are an estimated one million new children affected by divorce each year. If you add those whose parents remarry to the over 11 million children already in stepfamilies, you have many people trying to make stepfamilies work.

Brenda is a forty-year-old custodial mother, divorced a little over a year. She is thinking of remarriage to a divorced man. Her friend, Marla, suggests Brenda wait before remarrying. Brenda complains, "I'm tired of being a single parent."

Marla, who says she is very happy in her second marriage, replies, "Don't ever remarry to get help raising your children. Our biggest fights are over how to raise my children. Leo only saw his daughter once or twice a year. Living with my three teenagers on a daily basis hasn't been easy for him or for the kids. He wants to help me and tries to assume the father role. My kids don't want another father. They are happy to have me settle down again; but they don't want Leo telling them what to do. We've survived, but it hasn't been easy.''

Gretchen and Marla recognize the primary problem in a stepfamily. Gretchen would have trouble being mother to her stepchildren just as Leo has trouble being father to his. A stepparent who expects to move in and become a parent is bound to run into problems. Most children don't want someone other than their own parent as a parent figure in their lives.

Brenda, Ron, and Leo have the mistaken notion that children will love and respect someone just because their parent loves that person. They also think that since they love their spouse, they will have no trouble loving their spouse's children. Talk to any stepparent and they will tell you it doesn't happen that way. In fact, stepchildren and finances are the two major reasons why second and third marriages fail.

As Marla says, ''It isn't easy surviving in a stepfamily.'' Yet those who have survived the stepparent and stepchild roles tell how relationship skills made it possible. They offer some important advice for a stepparent and a parent who want to make a stepfamily work.

Stepparents:
• A stepfamily is not a natural family. It takes time to form bonds.
• Your stepchildren might still be recovering from the effects of their parents' divorce. Be prepared for disruptive behavior. Discuss with your spouse how to deal with this problem.
• Practice good communication skills; be a listener, a talker, and a TLCer.
• If your spouse is the non-custodial parent, make your stepchildren feel your home is theirs, too. If possible, set aside a room for them when they visit.
• Work out discipline guidelines with your spouse, let the children know that you both agree on these guidelines, and stick to them.
• If you have children of your own, go to a blended family workshop before you marry. If possible, bring the children of both families with you. After you marry, have family meetings to deal with the problems of blending two families.
• You don't have to love your stepchildren; but you must respect them and be kind to them.
• Don't expect instant appreciation for your stepparenting efforts. It might be years, if ever, before your stepchildren come to appreciate what you've done for them.
• Avoid making your spouse choose between you and the children. In most cases, you will lose.

Parents:

• Don't expect your children to love your spouse, but let them know they should be respectful.

• Don't triangle with your children against your spouse or with your spouse against your children.

• Be alert for signs of personality changes in your children. If necessary, get them professional help so they can learn to adjust.

• Show your spouse you appreciate the added burden of stepparenting.

• Let your children know you appreciate their difficulties and are willing to help them adjust.

• Don't let your children force you into a position where you must choose between them and your spouse.

A husband and wife must resolve to face stepfamily problems together. Making stepfamilies work calls for a commitment to practice family ties skills.

25

A Woman's Work
Is Never Done

The story of women today is quite different from the story of women forty years ago. Consider three women of the eighties.

Linda, who graduated from college in 1985, works for an accounting firm in New York. She enjoys her work and looks forward to advancing in her job as rapidly as the men in her company. Like most of her female classmates, she hopes to marry and have a family some day. She says she'd like two children. She also wants to continue her career, perhaps taking a break when her children are small.

Dolores, a thirty-five-year-old mother of three preteens, works thirty hours a week for a supermarket chain. Her income pays the additional mortgage costs on their new, larger house. She also contributes to a fund for the children's college education. Dolores feels lucky she's able to plan her work hours around her children's school schedule. Her only complaint is that she can't do the housework, take care of her children, and also enjoy some leisure time.

Christy works because she has to work. She is part of the word processing pool of a large company. She doesn't like the pressures of the pool. Yet she has no choice about working. Her husband is a steel worker who's been out on strike or in bad health for half of their eighteen-year marriage. When he's out of work, her salary is their only income. At other times, her earnings go to pay off debts accumulated when he's not working.

What effect do similar stories have on the American family of the 1980's? Is it harder to build strong family ties when mothers have interests outside the home? How do you build family ties with an employed mother in your family?

Gary Becker, a family economist, claims the American family changed more between 1950 and 1980 than in any thirty-year period since the colonial days. During this period, the rate of legitimate births declined, the divorce rate more than doubled, and the number of families headed by women tripled. At the end of the 1980's, over 13 million two-income families have school-age or younger children. Becker sees these changes as the result of the growth in women's earning power.

Women's changing role creates a family life much different from the family of the late 40's and early 50's, when many of today's parents were young. Even the mother who is not working outside the home is different from her counterpart of forty years ago. As a result, you have few proven models for how to make your family work in the 80's.

In some families, the advantages of both parents' working outweigh the disadvantages. Other families feel considerable pressure when both parents work. Family ties skills can help families deal with problems that may arise when mothers work.

If the mother in your family works, making the family work takes special effort. Your first step is to identify the advantages and disadvantages of a working mother for your family. Once you know what these are, you can use family ties skills to reduce the effects of the disadvantages.

Some possible advantages of a mother's working outside the home:

• Increased financial capability for the family.

• An opportunity for the mother to keep up with work skills she would want to use once the children are older.

• A chance for the woman to use her talents.

• A broadening of the mother's outlook, moving her beyond the confines of the home.

• An opportunity to make herself useful when the children no longer need her constant attention.

• A model for the children of a woman involved in many different activities.

Some possible disadvantages:

- Guilt for the woman who feels she can't live up to the standards of her unemployed mother.
- Stress from trying to be a Superwoman who is the best spouse, mother, and worker.
- Worry about whether the children are getting enough attention.
- Anger at the lack of flexibility in the work world.
- Indignation when other family members don't do their fair share.
- Tension when the house is disorganized.
- Resentment when other family members expect her to do everything.
- Frustration when family demands limit her ability to move up at work.
- Envy that family demands don't affect her husband's work but do affect hers.
- Less parenting for the children when the father doesn't share this responsibility.
- Less time to build marriage ties.

If you have a working mother in your family, you will find it easier to make your family work if you follow certain guidelines.

Develop a plan for managing the house. What is it that each person considers important for a well-run household? Respect each person's right to consider something important, even if you don't agree. Negotiate when one person seems to have too many demands.

Assign tasks to each family member. Each member should assume responsibility for chores according to interests and abilities. Divide up the chores no one likes to do.

Communicate. Everyone has to listen and talk when the mother no longer assumes that role for the entire family. Work on these skills.

Plan for some shared leisure time. When you and your family play together, you share ideas and concerns that might not come up at other times. Nurture opportunities to relax as a family.

Work on marriage ties. Don't overlook little problems because of time or job commitments. Work on your playmate skills.

Be flexible. Realize your plans will need to be adjusted based on changing interests and time demands. Be adaptable in times of crisis or celebration.

The way your family follows these guidelines will set an example for the next generation. You will be your children's model when they face the situation of an employed mother. Give them family ties skills, and they will know how to devise their own plan for making their families work.

26

A Man's Place Is in the Home?

Observing Lou with his infant son, Millie said, "Lou probably feels bad that Claire can nurse the baby and he can't." Lou believes in shared parenting. He went with Claire to the prenatal classes, took video pictures of the birth, and cuddled his son repeatedly during the first few hours after birth. After Eric came home from the hospital, Lou and Claire split all the child care tasks equally. The only exception is that Claire nurses the baby.

Claire and Lou both do freelance work, so they have flexible schedules. Lou feels that by the time Eric is two years old he will have mothered his son as much as Claire has. He also feels good that he is more involved with his son than his father was with him at that age.

However, Claire grumbles about Lou's behavior. She wonders how much of his shared parenting is for show or for his own satisfaction. She's upset because caring for Eric is the only work Lou shares with her. She continues to do most of the housekeeping chores. Lou believes in sharing equally but never finds the time to do more than care for Eric. In addition, Lou doesn't notice Claire's unhappiness. He thinks their sharing is complete.

Lou is an extreme example of a man who feels pressured by the changes in family life. Many other men also experience stress and are uncertain about how they are expected to act in today's world. Most adult men of the 1980's grew up in families where roles dictated behavior. Women cared for the home and nurtured the members of the family. Men fought the battle of the work world. Even those young adults who grew up in homes where these stereotypes weren't encouraged soon met friends who embraced these ideas.

The comic strip *Sally Forth* captures the dilemma of a couple committed to shared homemaking. Much as they want to distance themselves from the stereotypes of their youth, they often fall back on old expectations.

This is true especially for the man who wants to be an involved parent, a sharing spouse, a non-sexist co-worker. He must struggle to identify and then eliminate what is often unconscious behavior. He feels frustrated when he finds himself on the defensive with women who won't tolerate any expression of past sexual stereotypes.

Gene tries hard to avoid being sexist. Yet he complains that some women challenge every minor slip in a man's behavior. If he refers to the clerical help in the office as "the girls," other women accuse him of being a sexist. If he makes some reference to expecting his wife to do the wash, he's charged with exploiting her. He thinks he deserves some credit for honest effort most of the time. "What do women expect of men?" he wonders.

Just as there are no role models for how to manage a home with an employed mother, there are no models for how a husband and father becomes involved with home and family. Women often find the demands and politics of the work world puzzling. For men, parenting and homemaking are equally mysterious. A challenge for families in the 80's is to discover how men and women can share the secrets of those worlds that used to be only male or only female.

Men know they can survive in the work world. They are less certain about managing in the home. Part of the problem comes from women's previous monopoly on parenting and homemaking. Most women, even those working in a man's world, can't pinpoint exactly how their husbands could share in the traditional work of wife and mother. If making your family work means having a husband and father more attuned to life in the home, then you and your spouse ought to examine two important questions.

What's involved in homemaking? The traditional housewife performed a centering role in the family. She kept the home a place where family members could be at peace in the midst of a chaotic world. Family members knew their basic needs for food, shelter, and clothing would be satisfied in this peaceful center. The homemaker would take care of them. She cooked; she cleaned; she washed clothes; she ironed; she baked. She provided a comfortable shelter no matter what the family's financial resources.

The traditional housewife took care of the home and took care that it was a place of rest for its inhabitants. She was proud of her homemaking skills and passed them on to her daughters, largely by example. It often appears that these skills are instinctive for a woman, but here, too, children learn from the example of their parents.

Family members of the 80's, including mothers, still need this centering place. While your children are young, you and your spouse must work out a homemaking plan. You must consider what qualities will make your home a place where all will feel a centering peace. Then, you must agree on how to share the responsibility for creating this centering place. When the father realizes that his family needs centering, he begins to see the importance of his contribution to the family's home life. You need family ties skills to work out a plan in which both you and your spouse are "home makers."

What's involved in parenting? Some observers of today's families maintain that shared parenting isn't working. They say there is less parenting when a mother works because fathers are either unwilling or unable to share this role.

Actually, traditional parenting required both fathering and mothering. The child needed the centering given by the mother. The child also needed the opening to the outside world provided by the father. Now that mothers also work outside the home, fathers need to learn how to share the mothering tasks of parenting.

You and your spouse should talk over your ideas about how good mothering contributes to the family. To see the value of mothering, share stories about how you were mothered. Talk about what you think was missing in the way you were mothered. Since you had different mothers, you probably have different ideas about what's important. Still, you ought to be able to agree on certain essentials.

Decide what each of you must do to see that your children have this essential parenting. Periodically, review how you both are doing, perhaps trading responsibilities from time to time.

Today's man has a place in the home. Today's woman must help him find that place. Your family will work better if you and your spouse make a home together.

27

What About the Children? - Part II

The obstetrician's nurse overhears the mothers-to-be comparing notes. She doesn't envy them as they discuss baby-sitters, day care, and bringing the baby to Grandma while they work.

She says, "It wasn't as hard for me with my ten children as it is for mothers of one or two today. They have so many problems making child care arrangements. I can't imagine going through their ritual. I'd be exhausted by the time I got the kids to day care and myself to work. Then, they have to pick them up and deal with dinner, bedtime, and housework."

"Their biggest concerns are really about finding the best child care. They research child care arrangements just sitting in the doctor's office, asking each other for tips. They don't think there's much in the way of good care. Still, they keep looking for a magic place or person that promises to be a good parent substitute. I'm glad it's not me out there looking.''

Over half the mothers of preschool children and one third of mothers of infants under one year work outside the home. The percentage of working mothers increases as children reach school age. Even when a mother works part-time, she must plan for child care. What to do about the children when a mother works is an important question for families in the 80's.

Jane Pauley of the *Today* show has the ideal arrangement for a working mother. She has a live-in nanny, her husband works at home, and her schedule allows her to be home during the children's waking hours. Ms. Pauley admits, however, that her flexible schedule and good income are not available to every working mother.

Arranging flexible work schedules is still a worthy goal for those hoping to make the work world more responsive to family needs. On a flexible schedule, you and your spouse could share parenting, continue to work, *and* still have time for each other. If this option is not available, you must evaluate the pros and cons for your family of various child care arrangements. Remember to reconsider your choice regularly. Evaluate its effects on you and your child.

Live-in nanny or daily housekeeper. About eleven percent of two-income parents use a live-in or daily housekeeper.

One person caring for the children in the home has advantages for both children and parents. However, the cost is beyond the means of most families. Also, the nanny often spends more time with your child than you do. Are you willing to share your parenting with someone else? Finding a nanny or housekeeper who shares your values and ideas on child rearing is not always easy.

Take to neighbor or friend. In ten percent of two-income families, the children spend the day with a neighbor or friend. In some instances, these sitters care for more than one child. Your expenses are less than having help in your home. However, transporting the child to another house can be an inconvenience.

Use relatives as sitters. Grandparents or other relatives care for the children in close to twenty-five percent of families with working mothers. Sometimes, the relative lives with the family. In other cases, the children go to the relative's home. Usually, your expenses are low and you feel more relaxed about a relative's values and ideas on child rearing. Problems occur if your sitter feels unfairly burdened by your request but doesn't express this feeling. Be an active listener when you use a relative as a sitter.

Day care center. The biggest problem for the almost ten percent of working mothers who use day care centers is finding one that meets their child's needs. Parents must also find a center whose hours coordinate with their work schedules. If you choose this option, check out the facilities as well as the philosophy of the owners and workers. Visit the center unannounced. Talk with parents of children in the center about their views on the care provided.

Nursery school. This option, used by about five percent of working mothers, works well when child care is a part-time need. You should evaluate the school just as you would a day care center.

Alternate work schedules for parents. The choice of nearly twenty-one percent of two income families, this option is good for family life only if it doesn't hinder marriage ties. If you both work full-time on different shifts, your family has little time together. When financial need leaves no other option, you must make time for each other and plan for family activities.

One parent works at home. Only eight percent of the families with working mothers use this arrangement. If your stay-at-home parent is able to care for the child *and* do his or her work, it could be your best choice.

Older child cares for younger ones. Whether this option, chosen by seven percent of families, works depends on the maturity of the older child and the ages and number of the younger ones. You must plan carefully for any emergencies. In addition, you and your spouse must work at being good listeners when you are home. What works well one month might not work well the next month. Be aware that the older child may feel burdened or the younger ones may feel mistreated. Hold regular family meetings where your children have the chance to talk about how the arrangement is working.

Self-care. The term "latchkey children" applies to about six percent of children of working mothers. The authors of *Alone After School: A Self-care Guide for Latchkey Children & Their Parents* prefer the term "self-care." Their book is useful for both parents and children when this option is being considered.

At a certain age, a child no longer wants the protection of day care or baby sitters. Also, parents might want to consider cutting down on expenses. In either case, you must ask if this child, no matter his or her age, has the maturity to be alone after school, on holidays, and during the summer break from school. Self-care puts an added burden on parents. You and the child must agree— in advance—on what behavior is acceptable and how the child will use his or her time. You must do routine evaluations of the child's behavior and ability to manage alone.

Undoubtedly, child care creates a lot of stress for families in the 80's. Remember to give serious thought to how your arrangements will allow you time to work on family ties skills.

28

We No Longer Need
Your Services

Merger, takeover, downsizing, cutbacks, closure, Chapter 11, relocation, strike—all are familiar words to the readers of financial pages. Many families are aware of the human casualties behind those words. The job loss they signify spells financial and emotional turmoil for a family.

Sometimes, whole communities feel the sting of unemployment. A psychological as well as an economic depression hits families directly associated with a closed factory. Before long, businesses that service these families begin to feel the economic pinch and either cut back or close.

In other instances, a few employees from every level of the company might have their jobs eliminated. Then, there are the times an employee loses a job for poor performance or because of the whim of a superior. In addition, there are people looking for jobs after completing school or a training program. Those lacking skills in high demand undergo the ordeal of many rejections.

Whatever the reason, job loss, even if it's temporary, causes a strain on a family. The unemployed person feels stress. So does the rest of the family. Good family ties skills come in handy from the start for a family experiencing unemployment.

Problems for the unemployed. A job is more than an income producing part of your life. A job also gives you a sense of your own worth. You feel you are a contributing member of society. Thus, a job loss means more to you than a loss of income.

Losing your job triggers a variety of emotional responses. You can't believe this is happening to you. You're angry at the unfair treatment you're receiving. You want to fight back at the person or company responsible for your dismissal. You might waver between being glad you're out of a bad company and missing the part you played in that company. You feel discouraged as the reality of unemployment and its toll on you and your family become apparent. You experience depression as days and weeks pass and you remain on the unemployment list.

Moreover, you worry about the strain on your family. Do your spouse and children consider you a failure? How will they react if you don't find another job immediately? Then, there are your financial concerns. How will you pay the bills? What happens when your savings run out? Will you lose your house? Your car? Will your spouse be angry if he or she must assume sole responsibility for the family income?

Suggestions for the unemployed on dealing with your family. Your family wants to support you during this time, but needs signals from you about your reaction to your job loss. Don't try to hide your feelings from your family. Be a talker now even if it's hard. Others need to know how you feel. Also, be a listener. Your spouse and children worry, too, wondering about what effect your job loss will have on you and on them.

Try to appraise your future realistically. Yet be honest with your family about any expectations for long-term unemployment. Share your job search plans with your spouse, letting him or her know how you feel about your progress.

Work out a financial plan with your family. Let them know what adjustments everyone must make during your period of unemployment. Expect that some members will have more problems than others dealing with these adjustments. Encourage your children to find creative ways to earn money to meet their needs during this time.

Problems for the family. When one member of the family experiences a crisis, the whole family feels the strain. If someone in your family is unemployed, his or her anxiety affects everyone else. Unemployment puts additional stress on family ties because it usually affects the family budget. If you have financial troubles already, unemployment can mean disaster. Since children usually aren't fully aware of the financial condition of the family, they become fearful about the future. In addition, the unemployed spouse's depression and discouragement can strain your marriage ties.

Suggestions for the family of the unemployed. Now is when respect, tender loving care, and family pride are most important. Your unemployed family member needs your support as he or she comes to terms with a job loss. Your cooperation during the period of unemployment is also important. Don't blame the unemployed for the job loss. Encourage him or her in the search for a new job. Be willing to make the required financial adjustments. Don't burden the unemployed with additional worries. Be sure to include him or her in discussions of how the family is managing during this period.

Questions and suggestions for the job hunter. Now is the time to evaluate what future there is for you in your present line of work. What other marketable skills do you have? What other jobs appeal to you? What training would you need for another job? Should you consider job counselling, where a professional would help you explore other job options? Review suggestions in *What Color is Your Parachute?*, a do-it-yourself job counselling book. Check your library for guides to jobs in your local area as well as other areas of the country.

If you want to continue in the same line of work, what

job openings are in the want ads? Who are people who might help you find employment? Seek out their help and suggestions. If you must go to an employment agency, pick one with a good reputation. Avoid agencies that charge you excessive fees or a large commission.

If no jobs are available in your area, would you consider relocating? What expenses would you have if you were to move? What effect would a move have on your family? Could your spouse also find employment in a new area?

Once you decide the type of employment you want and where you want to work, develop a job search plan. Approach job hunting as you would a full-time job, spending your normal working hours on your job pursuit. Be prepared for rejections. Periodically evaluate whether your job search goals are realistic.

A period of unemployment is always a strain on a family. Nevertheless, if your family works together at dealing with your job loss, you could emerge from this crisis with even stronger family ties than you had before.

29

Grandparents

Mick and Andrea, both in their late forties, work full-time at jobs they enjoy. They also lead a busy social life. In addition to spending time with their young adult children, they look after the needs of their elderly parents. They try to plan two vacations a year, one in the summer and one in the winter. Recently, they became grandparents for the second time. They are proud grandparents who delight in their grandchildren even though they have little time to spend with them.

George retired recently. He and his wife, Theresa, now have time to do the traveling they dreamed of for so many years. When they are home, they are busy with volunteer work. George also spends time working on his prize roses. They have six grandchildren. George and Theresa visit the two who live in another city once a year. The children visit their city once a year. Their daughter-in-law never gives the children a chance to spend any time alone with their grandparents. George and Theresa feel bad that they aren't close to these grandchildren.

They see their other grandchildren at least once a week. Sometimes, they baby-sit for them. Since they usually are busy on weekends, however, they don't sit as often as their children would like. Still, they enjoy the time with these grandchildren.

Today's grandparents come in various styles. Gone is the idea that every grandparent is elderly, retired, and with nothing to do but entertain grandchildren. Instead, people are uncertain about how to be grandparents. Also, parents aren't sure how they want their parents to grandparent. Memories of their own grandparents cloud expectations of new grandparents and their children.

The authors of the *New American Grandparent* show that grandparenthood, as a separate stage in family life, has been around only for about forty years. In the past, most grandparents didn't live long enough for their grandchildren to know them. Today, nearly all children can have a relationship with two or more grandparents.

At the same time, grandparents seem younger today than the grandparents people remember. In biological terms, they aren't. Still, the older age grandparents of today *act* younger than grandparents of earlier memory. So, just as in many other areas of family life, there are no models for the new style grandparent.

Yet families in the 80's still benefit from good relations between grandparents and grandchildren. Your parents play a unique role in your children's lives. What grandparent hasn't said, "It's wonderful to be able to spoil my grandchild for a few hours. I know I don't have to get up for the 2 a.m. feeding or worry about what time the car will be home after a Saturday night date. It's all the fun and none of the worry." Your children profit from this loving, undemanding acceptance. Your children learn to give love and acceptance in return, often providing their grandparents with a renewed interest in life.

Your children also learn about their roots from their grandparents. They have a chance to hear the wisdom of people who have survived many of life's ups and downs. This continuity through three generations helps pass on enriching family values and traditions.

Grandparents today are conscious they are different from earlier grandparents. They appreciate being younger in spirit than their predecessors. They feel better able to communicate with their grandchildren. At the same time, they know they have less authority in the family than their predecessors often enjoyed. Hence, they proceed cautiously in their relations with grandchildren.

You and your spouse set the tone for the grandparent-grandchild relationship. If you want your parents and your children to benefit from this tie, you must explore ways to encourage it. Family communication skills are once again essential. Let your parents know you feel they play an important role in your children's lives. However, don't try to make them fit your idea of how they should act. Instead, discuss how they see themselves as grandparents. Be honest about your own ideas on child rearing. Understanding your ideas helps grandparents understand your children's behavior.

Pay special attention to four obstacles that might decrease the possibility of good grandparent-grandchild relationships.

If you live a distance from the grandparents, you and the grandparents must make a special effort to build the relationship. Letters, phone calls, stories about Grandma and Grandpa, even video tapes, help children and grandparents feel close even when they are far away.

Too much interference by the grandparent can spoil the grandparent-grandchild relationship. Grandparents have a certain freedom to tell their grandchildren what to do. If they overstep the bounds, however, the relationship could suffer. If this happens, talk with your children and their grandparents and try to sort out the problems. Then help them work out a peaceful settlement to their differences.

Sometimes grandparents are elderly or ill and you don't want the grandchildren to bother them. Or you might be afraid of how your children would react to the feebleness of a grandparent. Even if an elderly person can't tolerate long stretches with a child, he or she might still appreciate the excitement of a grandchild's visit. A short visit by a grandchild might also be an enjoyable distraction for an ill grandparent. Check out the feelings of the grandparent before you keep your child away. Visiting an elderly or ill grandparent, maybe even helping that person with small tasks, teaches your child concern for others.

A tragic by-product of divorce is the separation of children from their grandparents. Even if you feel hostile towards an ex-spouse, you shouldn't deprive your child of a relationship with grandparents. Try to work out a way for them to visit one another. Communicate with the grandparents, making sure they put aside any ill feelings toward you when they visit with your child. Make it clear that you welcome their interest in the child as long as they don't contribute to the upheaval the child is experiencing.

Encourage the relationship between your parents and your children when the children are young. As they grow older, they will cherish this link that strengthens family ties.

30

Planning for the Golden Years

Everywhere you go, you see retired men and women. They're in the shopping centers during the day. Or they're at the bank or the cleaners or taking a leisurely walk while most people are working. You see them at resorts, on cruises, on European trips, and in all the warm spots during the winter months. You see them wandering city streets alone. Some of them are still youthful and active. Others are elderly and ill. Some seem happy. Others are crabby. Some married couples still seem in love. Others are fighting over every decision.

You hear stories of people who scrimp and save for their retirement only to drop dead soon after they retire. You hear women whose husbands have just retired complain about having a man around the house all day. You see elderly people whose children never visit them. You know people who are saving for retirement, planning where they will live even when they are years away from retirement. You watch the expanding army of retired people and worry about your own aging. You wonder whether retirement is a blessing or a curse.

Then you see a president in his mid-seventies. You hear Bob Hope or George Burns. You read about Georg Solti conducting the Chicago Symphony. Or you remember that Michelangelo designed a church when he was eighty-eight. Grandma Moses was still painting at one hundred. Picasso was drawing at ninety. Adenauer was chancellor of Germany at eighty-eight. And Coco Chanel was head of her own fashion house at eighty-five. Long after "retirement age," Congressman Claude Pepper and activist Maggie Kuhn are busy fighting for the rights of the elderly. You see people in your own community leading active, productive lives well into their eighties. They inspire you as you plan how you will enjoy life in your golden years.

A college course entitled *Aging: a Process of Life* teaches that your retirement is simply part of a continuing process in your life. You won't be a different person after you retire. Instead, you'll live your retirement years based on how you've lived up until then.

People who enjoy their retirement years share certain characteristics that they developed before retirement. These people are, for the most part, satisfied with their lives, and they emphasize the good points rather than the problems. They feel good about their health, even when it is not as perfect as when they were younger. They are active with family and friends. They have adequate financial resources for their present and future needs, though they are not all well-to-do. They are independent, able to live alone and make their own decisions. In sum, the same qualities that make life enjoyable now will continue to make it enjoyable as you age.

Family ties skills, especially marriage ties skills, prepare you for making retirement work. Begin to plan now, not just for financial security and where you will live. Work at building your marriage ties. Then, you will enjoy that time in your life when you have fewer duties and responsibilities that take you away from your spouse. How you and your spouse relate now will determine how you relate later in life. If you don't grow together through the years, there will be no magical change when you reach retirement age. In fact, you'll probably disagree even more when you spend all your time together.

In addition to your marriage, you should examine five other areas of your life as you prepare for retirement.

Your work. Some people never stop working. Writers, artists, musicians, doctors, entrepreneurs, and politicians often continue to work years beyond the normal retirement age. Now is the time to consider whether you would continue with your work, even if you could retire. If you would, find out how you might continue your line of work once you reach retirement age. Perhaps you could remain in your job full-time. Maybe there would be part-time possibilities. You might start your own business. Or perhaps you could do similar work for a smaller company. You might also be able to teach your skill to others.

A second career. Some people find retirement gives them an opportunity to do work that has always interested them but which, for some reason, they were unable to pursue. Tim was in his mid-fifties, working at a job he didn't really like but staying on until retirement age. A recovered alcoholic, he spent many of his free hours counselling other alcoholics. A friend learned of an opening for a full-time counselor at a rehabilitation center. He suggested Tim apply. Tim and Alice reviewed their financial situation. They decided that, with a few adjustments, they could manage well on a slightly reduced income. Ten years later, Tim has no intention of retiring. He takes three months off each year so he and Alice can relax together. Sometimes, they vacation. Other times, they fix things around the house. One month, they worked at a friend's mission in a Third World country. Tim plans to pursue this second career indefinitely.

Health. An emphasis on wellness is critical if you want to enjoy your retirement years. Obviously, you can't prevent every illness. Some people have healthy genes, and others inherit a tendency to contract disorders that plague many older people. Still, if you follow the rules for good health now, you'll be more likely to enjoy good health well past age sixty-five.

Leisure time, hobbies, and volunteer activities. No one is sadder than a retired person with nothing to do. Watching game shows, soaps, and sporting events for twenty years is not a very appealing goal. If you have no hobbies or volunteer activities that enrich your leisure time, then now is the time to expand your interests. Without question, the happiest retirees are those who keep actively involved, not those who sit around doing nothing.

Family. If you're concerned about retiring, then work now at making your family work. Even the most independent retiree likes having good relations with his or her family. If you build family ties throughout your life, you'll enjoy the friendship of your children and your grandchildren when you are older. If you and your children practice good family ties skills, you'll all find it easier to deal with your process of aging. At times, your children will worry about you. With good communication skills, however, you'll be able to resolve any problems together.

31

Passing on the Dream

A *Cathy* cartoon captures humorously how families pass values from one generation to the next. In the first two panels of this particular cartoon strip, Cathy's mother describes how two different families spend their Thanksgiving weekends. One family writes Christmas cards. The other designs giftwrap for the gifts they spent all summer making. After each of these descriptions, Cathy and her father respond with a disgusted, "Bleah!"

In the third panel Cathy's mother sums up their holiday activity: "We spend the entire weekend eating." Cathy and her father respond excitedly, "Yeah! More pie! More pie!" In the final panel, as Cathy and her father devour the pie, her mother proudly says, "There's nothing like the holidays to define what's important to your family."

One reason you have children, either consciously or unconsciously, is because you want to keep alive what is important to you. As a parent, you wish to "pass on" what you have come to cherish as good and worthwhile. So, you teach your children to distinguish right from wrong. You encourage them to be good citizens. You give them advice and a "philosophy of life." Perhaps you give them a religious identity. Seeing your children cherish what you cherish gives you the satisfaction of a job well done.

If you are like most parents, making your family work includes teaching your children "what's important." In the 1980's, your values often compete with other values held up to your children. The values of their friends, the movies, music, television, and even their educators often conflict with yours. These other values can also be very appealing. You need to identify what's important to you and work to make those values equally appealing to your children.

General Social Surveys polls of American adults in 1984 and 1986 show that parents have definite ideas about what they want their children to cherish. First of all, they want their children to be honest. Then they wish them to have good sense and sound judgment and to be obedient. They also think it's important that their children learn to be responsible and considerate of others.

Only a small percentage of parents considered the following values important: trying hard to succeed, being interested in how and why things happen, being a good student, getting along well with other children, having self-control and good manners, and being neat and clean.

You might agree or disagree with what these parents consider important. You might also cherish important values that weren't listed in the survey. Sometimes, you are very conscious of the values you want to teach your children. In most instances, however, you are like the family in the *Cathy* cartoon. You pass on what's important without even knowing you're doing it.

In addition to being a school for relationships, the family is a school for values. Your children learn what's important—your values—more by the way you act than by what you say.

The store sends you two of an item you ordered but only charges you for one. You keep both items, claiming it's the store's mistake. What are you telling your children about honesty?

Each week you make an effort to visit an elderly relative to do chores she no longer can do herself. What message do your children receive about consideration for others?

You moan about the political campaign. Then, on election day, you fail to vote. What example of citizenship do you give?

You attend church services on a regular basis, contributing both time and money to support the church's work. What importance are you giving to religion?

You work long hours to earn money for an expensive

car, the newest VCR, and designer clothes for your children. Which do your children learn is more important: time spent with family or material goods?

You have holiday traditions from your childhood that you continue to follow. What are you teaching your children about their roots and their place in history?

Almost everything you do in your family sends out a message about what you consider important. Your children pick up these messages whether you want them to or not. If you can identify what's *really* important to you, then you can work to insure that your actions reinforce your teachings. Decide what things you cherish so much you want your children to cherish them, too. Then, examine which family activities are a help or hinderance in passing on these values.

You can discover how you teach values to your children by examining your activities over a period of time—a week or a month. Think about what these activities suggest is important to you. You probably will discover values you never noticed. Some of these you will like; others you might not be proud of. In the latter case, you should work to eliminate false values you may have given your children.

If you follow the *Cathy* cartoon strip on a regular basis, you discover another important truth about passing on family values. Cathy is a young adult of the 1980's. Her parents worry because Cathy doesn't seem to cherish all the values they cherish. Both Cathy and her parents, however, try to pretend they accept each other's values—often with humorous results.

You learn from *Cathy* that all you can do is offer your children your dream of "what's important." They will chose to value some things you value. They will reject others. They will also find things that are important to them that aren't important to you. You probably will be disappointed, as Cathy's parents are, when your children don't cherish what you cherish.

Still, as you work at family ties skills, you'll learn to value and respect another person's right to be different. Once your children reach their teens, they begin to make choices that challenge you to act on this value. Don't view their rejection of your values as a rejection of you. And don't reject your children because you don't agree with all their values.

32

Mother, Make Him Stop!

When Lori went to meet her friend's two grandsons who were visiting from out of town, she brought each boy a small toy. Eddie, the two year old, opened his first. He was overjoyed with his Mr. Potato Head. Tommy, the four year old, eyed his brother's toy enviously. After he opened his propeller driven boat, he couldn't decide which gift was better. When he discovered the propeller worked in the bathtub, he finally decided in favor of the boat. At that point, Eddie began asking if he could take his Mr. Potato Head into the tub. Whereupon, to keep peace, the mother had to give both children a bath.

Every parent knows about the problems of jealousy between brothers and sisters. This is an age-old dilemma. Adam and Eve had Cain, who killed Abel because he was envious of the Lord God's praise of Abel. All parents of more than one child know what it's like to feel frustrated when their children fight.

What parent hasn't had to referee verbal and physical fights between offspring? What family hasn't had a family outing turn into disaster because one child became upset with a remark or a look given by another child? What parent hasn't had a child come crying because a brother or sister has been nasty? What parent hasn't needed the wisdom of Solomon to decide who hit whom first? What parent hasn't tried to settle a dispute over one child wearing another's clothes? At different times in history, brothers and sisters may have quarreled over different things, but the odds are that they had problems.

What's new in the 1980's is a better understanding of how unresolved envy between brothers and sisters carries over into adult life and adult relationships. Helping your children get along with one another now not only makes your family work, it also helps your children establish good relationships in the future.

The subtitle of the book *Siblings Without Rivalry* appeals to every parent of more than one child. The authors promise you will learn *How to Help Your Children Live Together So You Can Live Too.* Their simple suggestions for cutting down on children's conflicts are interspersed with parents' tales of typical battles. When you apply family ties skills to settle these disagreements, you discover ways to lessen their impact on family life.

Acknowledge you can't eliminate all bickering. Some rivalry between brothers and sister is inevitable. A young child has a limited view of the world, with the child at the center. The child looks with disfavor on any threat to this important position. Since the child's relationship world extends only to the family, a brother or sister is automatically a threat.

Parents affirm their child's importance. So, to children, your interest in one brother or sister means you aren't giving your full attention to another. The other children then feel deprived. They can't attack you directly. So they attack each other, gaining your attention in the process. Even if you spend hours trying to explain you've enough love to go around, your children will sometimes still be jealous of one another. Periodically, this sibling rivalry will lead to hostile behavior toward a brother or sister.

Your goal should be to discourage intense jealousy, hatred, or competitiveness among your children. You also want to create a family environment in which children learn that sharing pays off more than fighting.

Realize some of their hostile feelings are real. Remember your own childhood. Recall the times you were angry at unfair treatment from a brother or sister. Even now, you probably remember many times when your anger was legitimate. How did you react when your parents didn't understand your side of the story? Most likely, you also recall times when you created the problem but didn't get the blame.

Don't encourage unhealthy competition. Some parents encourage their children to compete by constantly comparing one to another. Usually these parents let their children know which traits they value by bestowing more praise upon the children who excel in these areas. It could be good grades or athletic ability or good looks or musical talent. If you respect each child's desire to be special, you must recognize and praise each one's individual talent.

Parents of large families marvel at how different each child is. Unfortunately, from the child's perspective, being different sometimes implies being inferior. If one child is a beauty and another a potential opera singer, the beauty will want to sing and the singer will long to be beautiful. When you compare one child to another, you add to this confusion.

You can't always be fair. Children must learn very early that life isn't fair. It's a fact of life that even the most dedicated parent can't always treat each child equally. You shouldn't go out of your way to favor one child. Nevertheless, there will be times when you give one more attention than another. Your children must learn to accept this fact.

Guard against bodily harm. Disagreements can get out of hand. If your children use physical abuse to settle an argument, stop them immediately. Often, children see physical combat glorified in cartoons, movies, and sports. It is portrayed as an appropriate response when one is angry. You must make it clear to your children that this behavior is unacceptable. Separate fighting children until they cool off. Then, discuss their behavior with them and suggest alternative solutions to their disagreement.

Guard against psychological harm. Name calling, put downs, mockery, teasing and other verbal attacks in children's fights should not be tolerated. "Names will never hurt me" is not true. Some of the most devastating memories of childhood quarrels are of verbal fights. If your children engage in bitter verbal attacks, look for reasons behind the hostility. Then, work out a plan for dealing with that problem, and outlaw nastiness in the family.

Teach your children other ways of settling disagreements. Children must learn to deal with disagreements peacefully. Adapt family ties skills to their level to help them settle their arguments. Show them how to be creative fighters rather than disruptive ones. Teach them to understand each other's needs. Help them learn to express their feelings and, at the same time, listen to what others are saying. Children's bickering won't disappear completely. Still, it doesn't have to cause constant disruption. Keep bickering to a minimum, and you will find making your family work an easier task.

33

The Aftermath of a Revolution

In the 1960's, some people proclaimed the arrival of a great sexual revolution. Not only was sex free of its link to reproduction, it also was free from demands for commitment. Women, like men, could enjoy sex without any responsibility. The Playgirl could take her rightful place next to the Playboy.

These particular celebrators of sexual liberation, women's liberation, and gay liberation predicted the end of sexual hangups. They believed that eliminating laws and rules about sexual behavior would free men and women from generations of oppression. Sex for pleasure, devoid of any other meaning, would be the norm. Then, problems linked to sexual behavior would disappear. This sexual revolution would once and for all determine correct human sexual behavior.

Some people have, in fact, benefited from new insights into the biology and psychology of human sexuality. Married couples are learning how sexual intimacy helps keep romance alive. Couples with sexual intimacy problems are receiving help at sexual dysfunction clinics. Men and women with fertility problems considered hopeless thirty years ago are now having babies. Parents know the importance of educating their children about sexuality. In these instances, the advances of the 60's, 70's, and 80's are a positive influence for building family ties.

However, when you examine the sexual scene in the 1980's, you still find issues that cause stress and strain for families. Often, the legacy of the revolution is sexual chaos rather than sexual maturity.

As evidence that the sexual revolution hasn't led to a society free of sexual hangups, consider the following:

• A September, 1987, report lists a total of 41,735 cases of AIDS in the United States since 1981. Of the 1010 cases in the Chicago area, only 400 people were still living. Along with genital herpes, this new plague is causing increasing concern about the consequences of casual sexual relationships.

• Unwed motherhood among teenage girls is high, reflecting increased pressure for early sexual activity. Also, of the over 1.5 million abortions a year, over thirty percent are for teenagers, most of whom are unmarried.

• Wives are catching up with husbands' infidelity rates.

• The generation that celebrated the sexual revolution

has a forty percent divorce rate by the time they reach their early forties.

• Incest, child abuse, wife abuse, teenage prostitution, and kiddie porn continue to flourish.

• Most advertising aimed at teenagers is based on the rationale that sex sells. *Seventeen* magazine for teenage girls preaches sexual responsibility while carrying advertising that encourages young girls to be seductive. Designers and retailers who want to reach teenage audiences put out ads with definite sexual messages.

• Singles bars are filled with men and women, many angry that AIDS and genital herpes are putting a damper on their sexual freedom.

• Men in their mid-twenties say, ''Why tie ourselves down? We should have a good time now. When we're in our thirties, we'll find younger women to settle down with and raise a family.''

• Women who postpone marriage and motherhood begin to panic when they reach thirty and sense their biological clocks ticking away.

When you look at sex in the 80's, you realize the liberators failed to appreciate the *human* side of human sexuality. Though the sexual drive is instinctual, the meaning individual people give to a sexual relationship varies. As a result, partners in a sexual encounter might have different expectations about the meaning of their relationship. Sometimes they are conscious of these differences. At other times, individuals might not recognize differences because they don't even understand what they want themselves.

Betty Lechner, a social worker, says of teenage sexual activity: Boys use love which they know little about to get sex which they know a lot about. Girls use sex which they know little about to get love which they know a lot about. In other words, girls want love and boys want sex. Similar expectations color much adult sexual activity.

Societal confusion about the meaning of sexuality makes it hard for people to know what sex means to them. Making your family work in the 80's includes educating your children about their sexuality. Even if their school has a sex education program, you are the most important teacher of sexual values. A school sex education program is never value free. Nevertheless, if you are sure what sexuality means to you, you can teach your children your positive sexual values. You do this by example and by discussion as well as by teaching facts about sexual behavior.

Some points to keep in mind when educating your children about sexuality:

1. *Human sexuality is more than sex.* As the American Medical Association's statement on sexuality points out, human sexuality ''...is an identification, an activity, a drive, a biological and emotional process, an outlook, and an expression of the self.'' In other words, you need to teach your children values and attitudes about being a human person with a body that has a power-

ful drive. The implications of this drive affect "...every personal relationship, ...every human endeavor, from business to politics."

2. *Sexuality education begins at birth.* You teach what it means to be male or female long before you teach the mechanics of sex. The respect you show to others teaches your children a respect for persons that carries over into "every personal relationship."

3. *Talk about sex when your child is young.* Many parents are squeamish about sex education. Yet, if you begin discussions when your children are young, they come to see their sexuality as a natural function. You also teach them to respect themselves as sexual persons, making it less likely they will need to manipulate others sexually.

Since sexuality influences every personal relationship, the family as school for relationships must be conscious of its attitude about sex. If you are uncomfortable with your role as sex educator, don't hesitate to seek advice about how to fulfill this important role.

34

A Rebel in the House

A priest who worked with teenagers for many years says repeatedly, "There are two things in life I'd never choose to be—a teenager and the parent of a teenager. The teen years must be the most difficult period in family life."

The teen years are a transition period for teenagers and their parents. Making your family work during the years when there are teenagers in the house usually requires extra effort.

The trauma of the teen years is a by-product of what psychologists call "the search for identity." As part of the growing up process, the teenager begins to ask the question, "Who am I?" Until this time, a child feels secure as a member of the family. Preteens rarely question who they are. They know they're members of their family. That's all that matters to them.

However, about the same time as their bodies go through dramatic physical changes, teenagers begin to question the role of family in their lives. They sense they are more than just members of a family. They want to be independent. Yet they still need their family. The conflict between these two desires leads to mood swings in teenagers. One minute, they rebel. The next minute, they want the family car to get where they can do their rebelling.

The teen years are an exercise in trial and error for the teen, making life difficult for both you and your teenager. Yet without the trial and error, your teen won't become an independent adult.

The journey from dependence on family to independence is more difficult for some teens than for others. Some rebel against everything for years. Others rebel over minor issues for a short period of time. In either case, you must deal with the disruption this rebellion brings into your family.

As a parent who wants to both help your teen and make your family work, you must:

1. *Know what's normal.* Rebellion is normal for a teenager. The teen culture of the 1980's—the music, clothes, television, and language—makes a statement in favor of rejecting parental culture. If you squelch a harmless rebellion, you set the stage for more serious rejection.

In addition, a teen goes through constant mood changes. One day, everything in the world is wonderful. The next day, a teacher is critical, and everything is depressing. Everyone, including the family, becomes the enemy. Because teenagers cherish secrecy, you often are in the dark about what causes their mood swings.

Actually, parents are in the dark about much of what is important to teenagers because the family no longer is the center of their children's lives. For teens, the opinion of their peers becomes the standard for judging behavior. Too much dependence on peers can hinder progress toward maturity. Still, the peer group gives teens the chance to make the initial break from the family.

2. *Learn to let go.* The hardest thing you must do during your child's teen years is to let go. Letting your child take risks is not easy, especially when you *know* the harmful effects of some decisions.

Letting go should be a gradual process. You, too, go through the trial and error of trying to decide when to let go of one control and retain another. A thirteen year old might have her curfew extended an hour. At sixteen, she can stay out past midnight on the night of her formal. At eighteen, she goes off to college, and you no longer have a say in the hours she keeps. A fifteen year old can take driver's education. A sixteen year old gets his license, but you still set the rules for the use of the car. At eighteen, when he buys his own car, he takes on total responsibility for its use.

You and your teens must work out a method for evaluating when it is appropriate to let go of different parental controls. Even though communicating with teenagers is difficult, encourage your teens to work with you as you make decisions on letting go. You must be an active listener to try to understand their situation. You also must encourage them to be good talkers.

3. *Stick to your values.* Teenagers rebel against their parents' values, but they need the security of knowing there are values they can embrace in the future. Your teen might stop going to church, claiming religious leaders are hypocrites. Yet, if you stop attending church services, that same teen will be upset. Maintaining your values with conviction helps your teens know that someday, they, too, will have convictions about their values.

4. *Encourage their idealism.* People who work with teenagers often comment on their idealism. Instead of fighting over their harmless rebellions, challenge them to act on their idealism. You might develop an avenue of communication that will eliminate your teen's need for harmful rebellion.

Parents who are experts at family ties skills still don't sail through these teen years without worries. Not all teenage rebellions are harmful. Yet you know your teens have greater freedom than you did as a teen. You worry about rebellions that could destroy your teens' chances for future happiness.

You know smoking, reckless driving, gangs, dropping out of school, and teenage promiscuity all bode ill for your teens' physical and psychological futures. Talk with your teens about the repercussions of these activities. Give them information about the consequences they face if they participate in these activities. Set family standards with respect to these behaviors, and clearly state penalties for failing to stick to these standards. By setting limits, you teach your teen to make choices and bear the responsibility for those choices. If your teen constantly rebels against these standards, then you and your teen would benefit from family counselling.

You also hear about substance abuse, eating disorders, and the increase in teenage suicide. Be alert to signs your teen is having extreme difficulty with the stress of the teen years. If you suspect alcohol or drug abuse, anorexia or bulimia, or suicidal depression, seek professional help immediately.

Although your teenager may sometimes cause tension within the family, he or she may also make you very proud. If you work at family ties skills, you can enjoy watching your child move toward independence. If you concentrate on this positive growth, you'll find much about the teen years that is worthwhile. You and your adult children may never want to relive the trauma of their teenage years. At some point, however, you can come to appreciate the happy moments.

35
New Adults in the Family

After raising five children, Bev and Ken looked forward to the empty nest. They remembered marrying and leaving home when they were in their early twenties. From that point on, their parents had no responsibility for them. They expected their children to follow a similar pattern, leaving them free to be alone again after thirty years of child rearing.

Bev and Ken never anticipated what they now call the return of the young adult. When their youngest son, Bill, graduated from college, he needed a car. With car payments and college loan payments, he couldn't afford to live anywhere but at home. His parents agreed he could remain at home "until he got on his feet." Six years later, Bill is still getting on his feet.

Bev and Ken aren't happy with Bill's life-style but they

don't know how to tell him to move out. "He's an adult," Bev says. "I don't think I can tell him what's right or wrong. Still, some of the things he does upset me. I think we'd all be better off if he lived on his own. Then, I wouldn't know what he's doing. I wouldn't have to worry."

Bev also is "helping out" their daughter Mary Lou and her husband. She baby-sits for her grandchild while Mary Lou works three mornings a week. The younger couple is saving for a down payment on a house.

In spite of these unexpected demands, Bev and Ken think they're lucky when they hear friends, neighbors, and relatives talk about their young adult children. One young woman with three children under four moved back with her widowed mother when her husband grew tired of fatherhood. Another friend's son wants his parents to help him raise his two preschoolers. His wife moved in with his office mate.

Other friends wonder if their children are ever going to marry. Or if they will ever be grandparents. Ken's brother and wife don't know how to deal with their daughter's "significant other." Bev's niece and her husband have jobs on opposite coasts and see each other once a month. Bev's sister worries about how commuting affects her daughter's marriage.

If you listen to enough of these tales, you begin to wonder if there's any good news about the young adult and family ties. You also wonder why young adults seem afraid of commitment, of marriage, of parenthood. What will the families of the future be like if these young adults keep turning to their parents to help them out of every minor crisis? Another question might be: are parents today too involved with their young adult children?

Actually, there are many stories of good relationships between young adults and their parents. Still, the 1980's are a time of change for young adults (a term loosely applied to those between the ages of eighteen and thirty-five). This change is due, in part, to the sexual revolution and, in part, to women's changing role. It is also a result of better-educated young people who want to advance in a job and move up the economic ladder. These new opportunities for young adults put a strain on family ties because neither parents nor young adult children have models for how to behave.

The young adult in his or her twenties often is continuing the search for identity well beyond the end of the teen years. This extended search has some points in its favor. When Bev and Ken were that age, they made life choices without considering how many years stretched out ahead of them. Today's young adults know that they may live twenty or more years after retirement. They are in no rush to make a commitment that will bind them for that long a time. They also have more options than their parents did.

Still, parents worry about their children's futures. Erica Fromm, a psychologist and hypnotherapist, advises parents to relax. "You parents," she says, "worry too much. Some people stay adolescent until they're thirty-five. Give them time." Parents who thought rebellion ended when their children turned twenty find it difficult to think they might have fifteen more years with a rebel in the family.

The authors of *Parents' Work Is Never Done* offer advice on how you can help your young adult children grow toward psychological well-being. They emphasize the importance of the communication skills of active listening, good talking, TLCing, and positive reinforcement. Parenting an adult who hasn't outgrown the teenage crisis takes even more work than parenting a teen does.

However, not all young adults are still in crisis situations. Your young adult might not need your parenting help anymore. Still, the young adult lifestyle has undergone enough changes in recent years to cause possible misunderstandings between you and your young adults.

Your young adult may have values that conflict with your values. It is difficult to work out a relationship where you respect your child, even though you reject his or her values. You want to be the expert, just as you were when your children were young. Your young adult children, even when they want to be treated as adults, sometimes revert to childish behavior around you. Bev, Ken, and Bill keep falling back into roles they played when Bill was a teenager. Bev and Ken are too involved in parenting well after the time their son no longer needs a parent. It's no wonder the family environment is stressed.

It might be hard for you and your young adult to realize you must work to restructure your relationship. You no longer are the all-knowing parent to the dependent child. You are the less- than-perfect parent relating to another adult who happens to be your child. Avoid slipping back into parental behavior. Encourage your young adult to avoid dependency behavior. Following this restructuring, you should be able to build a good adult relationship.

Life with young adults ought to be enjoyable. Seeing your children lead productive and happy lives should give you the satisfaction of a job well done. If you and your adult children are good at family ties skills, you ought to be able to celebrate that feeling of satisfaction with them.

A parent's work at making family ties work is never done. Still, by the time your children reach young adulthood, you want them to work with you as partners. Together, you'll all work to maintain a family that is "comfort in grief and joy in time spent together."

36

Talking about the Family Secret

The elderly woman in the hospital waiting room shook her head as she read the pamphlet from the reading rack. She turned to her daughter-in-law with a surprised look on her face. "It says here that alcoholism is a disease. I never heard that before. Did you?"

The woman's husband of over fifty years was a patient in the hospital, suffering from the ravages of a life of alcoholism. Their marriage and their children's lives had suffered because of his drinking habit. She had always blamed him for being a drinker. Now, she couldn't let herself admit his drinking was a disease. She was angry at him for being a weakling and getting drunk. This anger made it impossible for her to accept a physical explanation for his drinking problem.

Every family with an alcoholic knows how impossible

it is for an alcoholic family to be a family that works. Excessive drinking causes relationship problems among family members. At the same time the drinker is reacting to his or her own relationship difficulties. Thus, the alcoholic can't work at building family ties. The other family members are so involved with the alcoholic that they, too, lack the emotional energy to build family ties.

According to Rachel V., the author of *Family Secrets: Life Stories of Adult Children of Alcoholics*, the family of an alcoholic lives in a house of secrets. Members follow a rule that says, "Don't talk, don't trust, don't feel." Family members don't talk about the alcoholic's problems. They also learn not to talk about their own feelings. As a result, all the members of an alcoholic's family carry the scars of the illness.

Some facts about alcoholism and about its effect on families:

• Alcoholism remains the most serious drug abuse problem in the United States. According to a 1985 Harris poll thirty-two percent of Americans report a drinking problem in their family. There are indications that alcohol consumption is on the decline in the 1980s. However, experts estimate the country still has at least 10 million alcoholics.

• Studies of alcoholics reported in the *New York Times* find that, in at least half the cases, heredity plays an important part in the disease. Children of alcoholics are four times as likely to be alcoholics as those with no family history of the problem. Even people with one alcoholic grandparent are more likely to become alcoholic. Alcoholism is a chronic, progressive disease.

• Families of alcoholics often deny that the afflicted member has a problem. Their refusal to confront the problem makes it impossible for them to deal with its effects on the family.

Alcoholism researcher Stephanie Covington discovered a strong relationship between alcohol and domestic violence. Alcohol plays a role in forty percent of family court problems. Eighty to ninety percent of battered women report their husbands have been drinking. Fifty percent of incest victims come from alcoholic homes.

If you are part of an alcoholic family and want to fight the ill-effects of the disease, then your first step must be to admit there is a problem. It is very painful to talk about this family secret and its harmful effects on family members. Nevertheless, you must first acknowledge the problem if you want to eliminate its power over all your relationships. Since everyone in your family is skilled at denying the problem exists, you might be the only one willing to admit there is trouble. You can still take advantage of the programs geared to helping you recover from the effects of alcoholism. Become a model for others in your family who eventually might follow your example.

Help for the alcoholic. The first of the twelve steps of Alcoholics Anonymous is to admit that you are powerless over alcohol and that your life has become unmanageable.

Alcoholic Anonymous groups, residential treatment centers, and outpatient programs throughout the country offer support for anyone who wants to fight alcohol addiction. If you want to stop drinking but don't know where to turn, ask someone in AA what options are available in your area. Depending on your condition, you might need residential care as you go through withdrawal from alcohol addiction. Follow-up treatment might include counselling or participation in AA. Either way, the road to recovery will be difficult. You also must rebuild relationships with members of your family. Most recovered alcoholics know they need the lifelong support of others who are struggling with similar problems.

Help for the spouse. Life with an alcoholic is never normal. You spend all your emotional energy reacting to your spouse's drinking. If you want to understand how your spouse's drinking controls your life, consider attending at least six Al-Anon meetings. Al-Anon is a self-help recovery program. It gives you the support you need to talk about your life with an alcoholic. Once you realize how alcohol affects your life, you begin to control your reactions to your spouse's drinking. You, too, have a long road to recovery as you struggle to change habits of many years. If your spouse is involved in a recovery program, consider marital or family counselling.

By participating in Al-Anon, you'll also become familiar with programs that will help your spouse if he or she finally admits to a drinking problem. You might also find the strength necessary to begin an intervention process with your spouse. In intervention, a skilled counselor helps you and your family force your spouse to admit to an alcohol problem. The most famous case of a successful intervention involved Betty Ford and her family.

Help for the children. Children are double victims in an alcoholic family. They lack the support of the drinking parent. The other parent not only can't support them, but often uses them as an emotional substitute for the spouse. There are at least seven million children living in alcoholic homes. Once they reach the age of twelve, they can participate in Alateen groups geared to helping teens who live in alcoholic homes.

Since the 1970's, increased attention has been focused on the problems of adults who grew up in alcoholic families. If you are an adult child of an alcoholic, you probably never had a normal childhood or the continuing support of your parents. Your adult relationships often suffer from this lack. You should consider joining an Adult Children of Alcoholics group, which focuses on "healing the inner child and learning how to reparent oneself." This group would support you as you try to build healthy, stable relationships.

Making your alcoholic family work will be hard. Still, once you begin to talk about the family secret, you can get help with it. Then, you will be in a position where you can begin to develop family ties skills. Don't let your family secret keep your family from being one that works.

A Not So Final Word

In the 1970's, some so-called experts claimed that the final word on the family was that it was an institution on its way out. Family sociologist Mary Jo Banes argued against this popular theory. In her book *Here to Stay*, she presented convincing evidence that the family is indeed here to stay. Even when Americans are unsuccessful at marriage, they don't give up. They try again, forming new families.

She didn't argue that families would be trouble-free, only that the institution would survive. Those who proclaimed the final word on the family were wrong. All that could be said both then and now is that families change in response to external circumstances. Dealing with the changing face of the family when there are no established models is the challenge of the 80's.

Some critics still argue that the family has no influence as an institution, and that it is on its way out or should be on its way out. They point to the following signs as evidence of that demise:

• Fertility experiments that make reproduction possible without the partners ever meeting.

• The high divorce rate and the resulting weakening of parent-child ties.

• Increasing numbers of couples living together instead of marrying.

• Problems of homeless teens, the throwaway children of our day.

• The decrease in quality parenting because of working mothers.

• The continuing problems of wife abuse, child abuse, and incest.

• The inhibiting influence of a rigid family.

• Generations of families on welfare.

• The increasing influence of peers and the media on teen values.

• School clinics prescribing birth control for teens without parents' permission.

• Teenagers obtaining abortions without parents' knowledge.

• Disappointing family relations that lead people to tell advice columnist Ann Landers that they would not have children if they had the chance to repeat their lives.

• Men and women who responded to a poll on marital

satisfaction by claiming that they would not choose the same spouse if they were to do it over again.

The critics are correct when they say there are many social problems that the family isn't solving. However, they neglect the data that show the continuing influence of the family. If they expect the family to do everything, then they are right that it is not succeeding. Families in the past never met all the members' needs, either, nor will families in the future. And yet, if families in the present learn how to foster good relationships, they will be building a strong base for families in the future.

Today, some parents and spouses are disappointed because their family relationships have broken down under the stresses and strains of the 80's. We can't be certain that parents in earlier generations didn't feel similar disappointments. There is historical evidence that many spouses did. Still, it is possible people are more aware of alternatives today and, therefore, more likely to express their disappointment.

Joyce Maynard, a columnist who writes on domestic affairs, suggests that her generation of baby boomers have been led astray by expectations of a perfect life. She surveyed her readers to learn what they thought about extramarital affairs and heard the excuse, ''You only go around once. Don't I have the right to make the most of the one life I've got?'' Her readers felt they had the right to fulfill all their emotional needs and live up to their potential for happiness. If they weren't meeting these expectations in their marriages, they then felt an affair was legitimate.

Those parents of baby boomers who say they wouldn't have children if given another chance have also been led astray. Their children didn't live up to their expectations. Yet when you expect near-perfect children, you are bound to be disappointed. Moreover, family life, like the marriage relationship, goes in cycles. There are ups and downs, with the downs often blocking out the memories of the ups.

Don't allow despair to be the final word on your family. On those days when you are grieving over a family problem, review the list of your positive family experiences. Use this list as an incentive to work harder at making your family work. Periodically, you'll need to celebrate the triumphs of the ups to diminish the impact of the downs.

The family experiences described in this book make it clear that you need effort *and* skill to make your family work. It is not enough to want to belong to a family that works. You also need to develop the skills to help you achieve this goal. Once you have the skills, you can apply them in different family situations. You'll soon realize it is impossible to be successful if you concentrate on only one problem area. You need to attack many different problems; but you also need to emphasize many different strengths.

If your family works together at building family ties, you'll be rewarded by enriched lives. The following are signs of hope that families can work:

- A five and six-year-old being kind to their ten-year-old brother who suffers from cerebral palsy.
- A wedding where brothers and sisters pay tribute to the bride and groom.
- Adult brothers who had their fair share of rivalry growing up now playing handball together on a regular basis.
- Young adults caring for an aging grandparent.
- A teenager who *offers* to cut the lawn.
- A family spending Thanksgiving at a food kitchen for the elderly.
- A doctor and his college-age daughter spending the Christmas vacation at a clinic in the slums of Puerto Rico.
- A husband and wife rejuvenating their marriage during an escape weekend.
- Children cheering up their dying sister.
- Parents sitting through a dance recital.
- A family at the zoo or the park or the museum.
- A preschooler helping his Grandpa milk the cows.
- Adult sisters visiting a sick, widowed brother every day of the eleven weeks he is in the hospital.
- A parent who lets go of a teenager.
- The proud parents of a new baby.
- The equally proud parents of an adopted baby.
- A family celebrating a religious holiday.
- Parents and stepparents helping a daughter celebrate her wedding.
- A daughter learning her mother's favorite recipes.
- A mother making her daughter's wedding dress.

- Brothers and sisters sitting through a brother's four-hour graduation ceremony.
- A sister cheering up a brother who is down in the dumps.
- A parent apologizing for misjudging a child.
- A husband and wife making up after a fight.
- Parents and their teenage son struggling through an argument—and then reconciling.
- A rebellious teenager who matures into a respectful young adult.

The constantly changing face of the family means that no suggestion for making a family work can claim to be the final word on family. Still, family ties skills should be helpful when facing any family problems. In addition, family ties skills keep you alert to the positive experiences in your family.

Your family as a school for relationships might never be the basis of a hit television series. It may, however, provide you with hours of happiness and comic relief. Your success at building family ties will determine how well your family copes with the downs and enjoys the ups of family life. Your work will help your children and grandchildren deal with the challenges of the next century.

The debate on what is the final word on the family probably will continue. Those who follow your example, however, will guess the secret: There is no final word, only a continuing need to work at making family work.